My Journey Begins Where the Road Ends

Readers are encouraged to go to www.MissionPointPress.com to contact the author or to find information on how to buy this book in bulk at a discounted rate.

Published by Mission Point Press
2554 Chandler Lake Rd.
Traverse City, MI 49686
(231) 421-9513
www.MissionPointPress.com

ISBN: 978-1-943995-28-8
LOC: 2017907470

Printed in the United States of America.

MY JOURNEY BEGINS WHERE THE ROAD ENDS

Thomas Ford Conlan

CONTENTS

CHAPTER FOUR

Home from the Sea

Finish every day and be done with it.
You have done what you could;
some blunders and absurdities no doubt crept in;
forget them as soon as you can.
Tomorrow is a new day;
You shall begin it serenely
and with too high a spirit
to be encumbered with your old nonsense.

— Ralph Waldo Emerson

DERBY DAY

The bluebird spoke to me from the fencepost
unable to see
      the hidden hole,
      his house turned to the barn
      by the winter wind.
I climbed down from the tractor
      turned the bluebird's house
      toward the morning sun.
He thanked me, whistled, and chirped.
I told my friends,
      as we watched the Derby,
      first I saw an oriole,
      then a bluebird spoke to me.
Doc said we'll have to watch him,
      I think he's crazy.

PROLOGUE
SANDHILL CRANES AND WINE

G hosts came to visit the farm on a past September morning. Three Sandhill cranes landed, framed by the fading grey oak of the pasture fence. The cranes moved slowly across the paddock out beyond the grape arbor, and loomed tall over the dying weeds and hay grasses. With lovely feathers, the birds stayed and grazed for what seemed a long time, though their gaze remained cautious toward the house. I let Stella, our shepherd, out the front door for her morning rounds. She circled the house, yet the cranes kept calm, drawn to the sweet, low-lying alfalfa. I wondered, perhaps Stella cannot see the birds, or perhaps their soft, ghostly grey blended with her black and white view of the world.

A summer-long drought followed the strangest spring weather I can remember. Ninety degree days in March caused fruit trees to bud far too early. A seasonable, yet heavy late spring snow nipped life from the fruit buds. The weight of the wet accumulation tore limbs, and broke orchard keepers' hearts, along with their pocketbooks. Notwithstanding, an abundant spring flowering allowed us a brief glimpse of the glory of years past.

I keep a small row of assorted fruit trees along the drive. The Macintosh apples normally bear fruit, though the deer claim most. Two peach trees have been productive over the years, but both lost large limbs from the weight of the spring snow. With the exception of a few plump peaches, the trees, though leafed out, were barren of fruit.

A year ago in the spring, I planted two new hybrid apple trees by the pasture fence to replace a perfectly formed mulberry tree lost to disease. The mulberry had been our favorite, the juicy, black berry fruit especially enjoyed by our three grandsons. We never quite got around to making mulberry jam because berries somehow disappeared right off the tree. The mystery of vanished fruit was solved with little detective work, as purple stains dotted the white tee shirts worn by Zeke, the middle boy, and Walker, the youngest. The oldest, Grady, naturally told on his younger brothers, though I suspect that he also participated in a free-for-all berry fight. Mulberry juice disdains the effort of modern washing machines.

Then a year came with no fruit. The sweet wood invited pests inside the bark. We watched helplessly out the back window while woodpeckers throttled the mulberry by pecking rows of perfectly aligned holes to capture hidden bugs.

In mid-August I noticed the two new apple trees being affected by the dry season. A small fir tree, planted in the spring, behind a row of healthy blackberry bushes, also cried for a drink of water. I put the drip hoses out and hoped.

After Labor Day, with rain finally in the forecast, I fertilized all the trees. This year's harvest was lost, but in the growing business "next year" always gives hope. The sun came out, then hid with a musical beat, as I pounded the fertilizer stakes deep around drip edges. Rolling clouds and a few sprinkles of rain slowed the process only slightly, and soon I finished. A muscle twitch portended an ache, which I soothed with a drink of cool well water, and rest in a soft chair by the woodstove.

As I sat and recovered, I pondered the grapes growing sweet on the arbor built from cedar saplings. The arbor has filled with carefully tended vines. In good years, the vines have produced enough grapes for two or three dozen bottles of wine, and several cartons of canned jelly. Trimmed back and formed each March, the vines return healthy, and flourish with leaves through the summer. Buds appear on the purple brown virgin boughs, and one day, without notice, small and gentle fingers of fruit, on tiny bright green stems, sprout from pinkish flowers.

This year's grapes had started out well, apparently not affected by the spring snow. In June, I fought my annual battle of conscience, whether or not to spray the vines with pesticide. Just once in the dozen year life of my vineyard, have I sprayed the fruit. The grapes flourished that year, but I always worried; about the birds, about tainted wine, about my family and friends eating grapes from the vine, though I always warned them to wash first. I chose not to spray, to take my chances, trusting nature to take my side.

In July, I began to notice birds fluttering in the vines. Thankful I hadn't sprayed, I enjoyed their comings and goings through the deep green leaves that camouflage the cedar arbor. On the hottest of summer days, walking the aisle beneath the leaves is much like entering an air conditioned room.

But when August arrived, many of the hopeful fingers of fruit were gone. I fretted over the loss and hoped September would leave just enough for a modest vintage.

❧

Around midday, the sun came through the clouds, and beckoned me back to the arbor. Grapes grown sweet waited to be crushed into wine before autumn arrived.

The cranes looked on as I picked surviving grapes by hand. Carrying a large pot, I set out to the arbor thinking I might need to buy grapes this year, or maybe try using juice from a local fruit market. But I have never used someone else's grapes in my wine. I began to pick along the outer side of the arbor, the sun still out, and the wind freshening. I used a different method than in other years. I picked each grape individually or in strands of two or three, and carefully dropped the fruit in the pot. I found a few bulging bunches. My spirits rose. Working my way around the arbor, I pulled back leaves and beheld more and more of the juicy orbs hidden in dark, shady reaches.

The sky darkened as I turned under the canopy, the first pot almost filled. Raindrops hit the leaf ceiling above me, but underneath, I stayed dry. My fingers chilled like the grapes in the shade. As I reached, occasionally a grape was broken, and I tasted the fruit, thick and sweet. The rain hitting the leaves echoed, and drops continued when the sun returned, lighting the earth. I was transfixed by a sun that shone above an autumn shower.

After a couple hours, this year's crop lay in the pots. I had picked about ten gallons of promising fruit, and returned to the house, cleaned up the fermenting crock, and began pulling each stem away from each grape. I separated the first four pounds of grapes, and kneaded the fruit in a large bowl, squeezing with my hands, and smelling the rich sugary juice, as the grapes turned magically from fruit into liquid. I finished the first bowl. The crushed grapes were ready for the crock.

But what to do with my hands?

If I picked up the bowl it would slip, and break on the ceramic tile floor. Coveted juice would be lost. Instead, I licked the thick juice, first from my palms, then from the back of each of my sun tanned hands that tingled from the tannins in the fruit, and finished by licking each finger. The taste was exquisite.

Startled from reverie by an intense prehistoric croaking, a herding dog bark, and the whiny of the Haflinger pony out by the barn, I ran to the window curious, but seeing no cause, trotted barefoot out the door, and felt cool green grass in my toes. Three cranes soared high over the grape arbor, circled the barn and the pasture, and like angels having shed their ghostly grey masks, gracefully flew to the west over tall red pines, in search of water.

CHAPTER ONE

NOT A SAILOR BORN

FAWN

Popple leaves shimmer,
silver undersides cascade in the breeze.
A fawn hangs,
spotted, in tall grass,
suckling.
A doe stands awkward, alert, alarmed to a presence.
The wind carries a message, a warning, she listens.
A wooden screen door bangs.
With her eyes, her stance, she tells her fawn to hide,
lie low, safe in the grass.
She steps away, bony legs askew,
drawing danger,
willing the presence,
follow the wind away.

GRANDPA ARNOLD

In my last vivid memory of my mother, we touched hands while attendants wheeled her out of the house and into the ambulance. Her eyes glazed tired. Her hands too weak to grip. My mother would die in the hospital, and back then, hospitals would not let young children visit. Pop, frantic with disbelief, looked in through the window of the car in the hospital parking lot, where I waited. He was helpless, knowing I would never know her, never see my mother again.

My family spoiled me some as a result of my mother's passing. I was four when she died. My mother's sister, Aunt Emily, wanted to take care of me, maybe even raise me. Of course I would need a mother. So Pop, my dad, chose instead to send me up to the family farm to stay with my paternal grandparents for a while.

My mother had loved to visit the country, just as my Grandpa Arnold loved his farm, the quiet mornings, and the pungent yet prosperous earth. The two of them had a special relationship with the land not shared by my father.

I have an old picture of Grandpa in Detroit, in 1901, outside a brick garage at Woodward and Jefferson. His hat is tipped back. A cocky attitude stares out from beneath the brow. Grandpa worked thirty years as a street car conductor to buy the farm from his in-laws, the Newberry clan, my Grandma Ada's family. By 1936, Grandpa had saved enough and made it out, out of the city, and back to the simple earth.

Pop was living on his own by then, settled in a good paying job building tanks for the coming war. He was the older of two sons raised by my Grandpa Arnold and Grandma Ada. Pop was not suited to the country life. He was good with numbers, educated as an accountant, and successful in the civilized world of Detroit manufacturing. Pop had a passion for new cars and nice clothes. Never comfortable at the farm, he knew his way around the pavement of the burgeoning Motor City.

My father outlived and buried three women companions in his lifetime. My mother was the first, and his only true love. I never saw him cry.

Grandma made pies. And for me she baked a special one in a miniature tin. Blueberry, still my favorite, warm and butter crisp, a bite of pie melted in my mouth. I remember milk to wash the crust down, fresh from the bottle by way of the barn, and a swallow of cream floated on top.

Grandpa had an old Ford step-side pickup. Nothing fancy. Uncle Doug, Pop's younger brother who inherited the country gene, a gene since passed to me, once told me that Grandpa got over a hundred thousand miles on a set of tires. He never drove much over twenty.

Seldom used railroad tracks formed the Blaine crossroads, where Grandma ran the Blaine General Store out of the first floor of the farmhouse. Grandpa worked the fields, tended a few dairy cows, and raised a flock of turkeys. Grandma served locals as Postmaster, sold feed, grain and seeds, and a few basic necessities to get farmers by without having to drive to "Port." Port Huron, the big city to us, a river town, lay seventeen back road miles, or twenty-four meandering river miles downstream from the farm. Port Huron had been settled at the mouth of mighty Lake Huron, near the confluence of the Black and St. Clair Rivers, where only a rapid, blue current separates the States from Canada.

Grandpa expanded the farm to over six hundred acres, including a quarter-section bordering the Black River a half mile west of the farmhouse and store. At the edge of the plowed fields, a high ridge opened over the river valley two hundred feet below. Many years later, I inherited this piece of the farm. Often I would sit on that hillside, a grassy bank veranda, and dream, as I stared out over simpler times.

Five years old, and I climbed into the old Ford just out in front of the store. I wanted some more gum, and began to pout when Grandpa said no. He looked me directly in the eyes, and with his hands strong from the fields, drew his forefinger back against the meat of his thumb, and flicked my tender cheek, just once.

Grandpa's eyes spoke words he was unable to utter. I saw the pain of my mother's death in eyes I see each morning in the mirror; eyes I look through when I sit on the grassy hillside overlooking the river bend, eyes that weep yet cannot cry. I settled into the torn and rumpled leather seat, dispatched and alone, having learned the first lesson of an overindulged child.

Tears flow easily now through hardened emotions when from a safe distance I witness happy scenes or sad, on film or in life, though I never cry at death.

Grandpa died not long after my mother. Uncle Doug and Pop each inherited half of the farm, but Doug stayed and worked the land. Grandma Ada closed the store, and split her time between the farmhouse and the city. She lived with my family, helping Pop and my older brother Dennis raise my sister and me. My mother's death had affected my ten-year-old sister more deeply than we could know. Dennis matured too early at fifteen. Always positive, with a stoic intelligence, he was like a second father, a stable role model.

Grandma taught me to read and write before I entered kindergarten. She made a game of the teaching. Between lessons, Grandma would play Tonto to my Lone Ranger, then hug her "Tommy" with warm and complete affection, the way a mother might have.

✠

In the summer of 1971, tired of college, and the academic study of philosophy, I yearned for the real world, and searched for answers travelling through Europe and the British Isles. I walked alongside my Moped across the crest of the Alps, and gently touched the throttle. My motorized-packhorse weighed heavy with gear.

Imagining myself the great adventurer, I had hardly slept the night before, my senses dulled by a bottle of chardonnay, and a hasty meal of canned sardines and a baguette. Scared and humbled by an animal, maybe a bear, but more likely a raccoon rummaging through my campsite well before dawn, I jumped up from my sleeping bag into an overhanging tree branch. The limb snapped back, left a welt on my cheek, and a clear message in my mind. Grandpa's farm had worked for me as a child, so many years earlier, perhaps it could again be a place to clear the cobwebs from my head. I had become a child of many worlds, travelling the open road, through countryside and city. I yearned for a place to call home.

❧

Uncle Doug kept horses at the farm when I returned from traveling through Europe. I learned to ride that fall on Booger, a strong and wild bay gelding. He delighted in tossing me off after running uncontrolled back to the barn, his way of telling me I did not belong. But I fought his willful spirit, and always climbed back on.

I commuted to college at Oakland University, back in the Detroit suburbs, and scheduled classes so that I had to drive to the campus only three times a week. I attended school all day, then worked until midnight delivering pizza, and supplemented that income by driving a cab. But it was sixty miles each way by back roads between school and the farm. The pace wore me out within two months, and I discovered that I enjoyed the simple country life. I quit school and my jobs and stayed at the farm, pretty much broke. The old farmhouse cupboards held only teabags, Bisquick, and honey. I found solace from a ride on horseback, a bit of guitar, or a long walk to the river.

❧

Aunt Alice had grown up a farmer's daughter, and had waited for Uncle Doug to return from the South Pacific campaign in World War II. And he did come back, an understated hero. He never talked about the war, but without warning, his attention would wander, and his eyes, eyes he shared with Grandpa, and with me, drifted away into an empty sky.

Uncle Doug worked construction as a union pipe fitter, and had landed a good job building a power plant a few miles away. He still kept the farm going at a lesser pace. Helping him out kept me busy. I worked for my supper down at their place, a newer ranch Doug had built. Aunt Alice always cooked lots of fresh vegetables out of the garden, including buttered potatoes and sweet corn with every meal.

The late autumn evening in Michigan cools quickly, and I no longer could afford a car. Freedom can be defined by a walk in the dark on worn blacktop. At the end of most days, I wandered the half mile down the road from the old place to Doug's newer house. A pasture ran along the road. More than once I looked north over the pasture to watch the northern lights swirl like ghosts in the darkening sky. I found some peace in the knowledge that I looked over my family's land. But deep down I knew the land was not mine. Maybe someday, but I needed to earn it first.

I have since lost the assuredness of ownership, and have learned that land can only be borrowed. A fleeting, momentary peace may be found in understanding the earth and the sky and the water. I see old farms hidden beneath city streets. I walk in wonderment upon the natural earth, and believe in the good of the world, and the infinite power of nature.

⁂

Aunt Alice would let me have it when I made my own dinner at the old house. She'd say, "Having a clean meal, huh?"

I had to ask what she meant. In the old days, when Grandma was down in the city watching me, Grandpa would make his own dinners from time to time, too, rather than driving the old Ford down to her place. A "clean meal," he called it.

Doug had planted forty acres of corn on a field by the curve of the blacktop road. The plot was just across from Grandpa's old barn, which I had raided to panel the living room in the old house. Uncle Doug wasn't too happy when a strong wind toppled the barn roof, mostly because I'd created a skeleton by taking the siding. He asked, pointedly, "What the hell you doing, homesteading?"

In late November we combined the corn. The weather was bitter cold, and my soft hands felt like cube steak, and worked about as well. I was pretty good at driving trucks and other machinery, but had never driven a semi full with corn through a field of greasy mud and ice. I got her moving pretty well, when afraid of too much speed, let off the gas. The tires mired in. Uncle Doug, irritated but smiling, cranked up the old John Deere, and in the cold dusk we had to tow the truck to solid ground. His simple words, "That's just about enough for tonight."

The next day, while Uncle Doug worked back at the plant, I ferried truckloads of corn over to the elevator to be weighed, and then to the cattle farmer, who bought the feed corn. I was on the last load, in the borrowed truck that I'd gotten stuck the night before. Just short of the elevator, near the Wildcat Road, I shifted, heard a screech, then a clunk. The truck stopped.

I had screwed up the clutch getting out of the mud in the field. Not a big deal. I waited by the side of the road for the cattle farmer to come and tow the last load home with his tractor. I rode in the cab, and steered the truck while he towed.

Back at his farmyard, he used the tractor to ease the truck close enough to dump the corn into his crib. I got out and grabbed a shovel, figuring I would have to climb into the dump bed for the last bit of corn. He started the hydraulic lift, and I noticed my shovel resting against the side of the truck bed. I ran to grab the shovel, which was bending in an arc from the weight of the bed, and when I pulled, the handle popped free, and bonked me in the forehead.

A few weeks later, in early December, just before I left for the west coast, and my eventual enlistment, Alice asked me down to their place for Sunday dinner. My Uncle had been paid for the corn, according to the agreed upon price, one thousand dollars.

After dinner, Doug showed me the hand-written statement, a thousand, minus a hundred bucks for truck repairs. Uncle Doug didn't say a word, he just looked at me with my grandfather's eyes.

Another flick on the cheek.

HARDBALL

On every sunny Saturday morning I laid awake in bed, if for only a moment, to consider the wondrous possibilities of the coming day. In 1956, Pop had taken a job managing a plant that built tanks in Newark, Delaware. Living "out East," I lost touch with my Grandma and the farm, but discovered a whole new natural world, fishing creeks, and building forts, and in fighting friends and foes, most often the same person. And I found baseball.

Dennis and Pop volunteered to coach my Pony League team. Dennis had to help because Pop never played baseball. Pop, a big man, had played some football, offensive tackle. At forty-eight and carrying a lot of weight, he looked out of place with his red "Coach" tee shirt tucked in to wool suit pants. His leather wingtips shined.

Everyone made Pony League, the no-cut "minors" for real Little League. You had to be nine to try out for Little League, and hardly anyone made it until they turned ten. Some careers peaked in Pony League.

Coming from Detroit, one of the original six National Hockey League cities, I wondered at the name on our tee shirts, the Montreal Canadians. A hockey fan must have named the four teams, as we played the Maple Leafs, Bruins, and Rangers. No Blackhawks, no Red Wings.

The first practice came and we needed a catcher. With the other kids afraid of the ball, Pop said, "Tommy, your Grandpa was a catcher, why don't you try it?"

Somewhat awed by the gladiator outfit, I began by putting the right shin guard on my left leg. Dennis showed me how the metal clasps hooked on the outside. I put on the chest protector, then looked down at the rest of the gear that had been poured on the ground from the army-canvas bag. I saw what I assumed to be two masks. One had wire caging supported by soft leather pads which I knew would fit against my forehead and chin, and soften the impact of the hardball hitting the wire cage. The other was a small metal triangle with rubber padding around the edges, probably to protect my nose. I picked the triangle up and fit it to my face. When Pop and Dennis started laughing, I realized my error.

We lived in a new, brick split-level house that Pop bought in an upscale subdivision named Windy Hills, the first planned neighborhood in

Newark. About two miles out of town and surrounded by wooded hills and farmer's fields, I had a short walk through any neighbor's backyard to the wild.

My first best friend, Paul Chandler, lived two doors down. Paul played on the Maple Leafs. He and his dad were Yankee fans, the worst. I hated the Yankees, always first to my Tigers' second. Even then I knew their players' allegiance had been purchased by some rich New Yorker.

Our catches turned into full nine inning games. Al Kaline, Stormin' Norman Cash, and Rocky Colavito hit for me. Paul had Mickey Mantle, the upstart Maris, and Yogi Berra, a never ending lineup of home run hitters. The rules changed constantly so we never knew who won. As tension built, Paul and I found ourselves rolling on the ground, wrestling for the reputation of our teams. My temper usually started it. A day or so would go by until we shook hands, and got out our mitts for another game of catch.

We both turned nine and tried out for Little League. A couple of our older buddies around the neighborhood dominated the league. Twelve, and a lefty, Jack Mace threw heat and a nasty curve. Johnnie Marks, a catcher from across the street, was the best hitter in the league, except when he faced Jack. Paul and I were good, having gained experience in pickup games with these guys, but neither of us got picked.

Back in Pony League, something clicked. I started hitting the ball hard. Pop had given up coaching, and given a choice, I gave up the catching gear for the infield. During the first three games, I hit ten straight doubles. A few might have been homers if we had a fence like Little League.

A kid I knew from school made Little League, but never got to play. I went with his dad to watch a game. Jack was pitching for the Delaware State Bank Tigers, so a big crowd had gathered. A man sat next to me on the bleachers, and we started talking baseball. He asked, "Why aren't you playing?"

I told him I still played Pony League, and bragged about my hitting. He told me that he coached the Pirates. "I don't like to take kids from Pony league in the middle of the season, but one of my players moved out of town. Why don't you talk to your parents about playing for me?"

My pride popped out of my shirt when the coach called the next day, and Pop said, "OK."

Paul and I stood throwing the ball around in his front yard. A Newark City Police car eased up to the curb. The Officer opened his door and, smiling, walked around to the passenger side. My new coach, dressed for day work, reached into the seat, and handed me a gray wool uniform with blue piping that spelled out, "Aetna Hose, Hook & Ladder Pirates."

Paul stared and said, "Man, I wish I had gone to that game."

Paul made the Yankees the next spring. Sponsored by a new hamburger place in town, McDonald's, they had brand new, red and white uniforms. The whole team got free fries, a hamburger, and shake every time they won. Like their New York namesake, the Yankees always won.

By our eleventh summer, Paul and I had developed into two of the top players in the league. Paul caught for the Yankees, and I played just about every position for the Pirates. A strong hitter, my temper had grown even stronger. Still spoiled, the slightest provocation sent me into a tantrum. I wanted a hit every time I stepped to the plate.

Late in the season, with the Pirates down a run to the Yankees, I struck out with a man on second. In front of the bleachers, I flung my bat and helmet against the backstop, barely missed the on deck hitter, and let out a frustrated oath under my breath. As I walked back to the dugout, parents and families in the bleachers stared me down, aghast. Coach firmly directed me to the bench, and I hid the last inning in the dugout.

The Yankees won the league title, and Paul's coach, also the Minister at the Presbyterian Church Paul attended, picked the All-Star team to play against Wilmington. He picked the best three players from each team, and though I was the best fielder and hitter on the Pirates, he left me off.

Paul made the All-Star team. Playing catch in his front yard the next day, Paul looked down, "Coach said you're a poor sport."

Worse than a flick on the cheek.

WHITE CLAY CREEK

I remember the sound of crackling ice, the cold water rushing into my rubber boots, and my legs growing numb, before realizing I had touched bottom. I stood unsteady, and struggled to keep my balance. The current flowed between my legs. My mind entered a blank shock, and my upper body dripped. Several moments passed before the world returned to focus. I feared being pulled under in waist deep water, being carried downstream, and drowning, while I clawed at the underside of the ice covering White Clay Creek.

&

A couple of the guys in our gang, Johnnie Marks and his little brother Mike, had come by the house looking for a sidekick in childhood crime. An unseasonably warm day in late February called for a hike down to the creek bottom woods. Maybe catch a frog, or climb some trees to see who could reach the highest, sway the farthest, and swing from the upper most branch of a tall maple.

We walked down the street past Paul's house, not bothering to knock. His parents kept him over-protected, close to home. He "wasn't allowed" to play in the woods. I paused by the corner house just above the ridge overlooking a valley created by untold thousands of years of the flooding and receding creek. Debby Raymond lived on the corner. Her dad, Tubby, coached football for the University of Delaware Fighting Blue Hens. Debby, a bit of a tomboy, kind of liked me. I felt a sharp pain in my backside, and saw a small rock bounce off the sidewalk. Johnnie, two years older, yelled, "C'mon Conlan."

We climbed down the steep ridge, tripped on exposed roots, and slid on patches of loose dirt. Walking to the end of the block to take the winding two track path would have been too easy.

At the bottom of the ridge, a grassy flat had been cleared out into an open area, our makeshift neighborhood ball field. Crusty snow and ice outlined the backstop built from wooden posts and chicken wire. Come spring our thoughts would turn to pick-up games. If you hit the woods in the air, it was an automatic homer. But then the game got delayed or maybe postponed, while both teams kicked through the underbrush looking for the ball. By the end of summer, all the new leather baseballs had been lost. The game couldn't start without a search of the woods, and a roll of black electrician's tape to keep the found balls together.

A couple hundred feet into the woods past left field, Johnnie Marks, the toughest guy in the neighborhood, built a tree fort. The fort belonged to Marks. He owned it. Anybody climbing up without Johnnie's permission paid dearly. Perched like a hawk's nest in the spreading branches of an oak, the fort had an all-around view of the clearing below. No enemy could approach unseen.

The wooden slats nailed into the tree to serve as ladder rungs had worked loose, unused over the winter. We climbed anyway, teetering up and down as we stepped, and hoped the nails wouldn't give way. Marks had cut a square access hole through the plywood floor. The plywood had been donated by neighbors we didn't yet know who were building a new house the next street over. Like Texas Rangers, we sat thirty feet in the air, and guarded over all we could see.

Mike whined, with his head cocked-up, when Johnnie wouldn't let him climb into the fort. Johnnie picked on his little brother, but nobody else could. Johnnie reached into a metal box hidden in the crotch of the tree and pulled out a match. From his pocket he drew two Winston's taken from his mother's purse. After a couple of puffs, my lungs burned and I felt a little dizzy, but I talked tough while fighting off a cough.

Looking out between bare tree trunks, we saw Mike, head hanging down, walking toward the creek. I called out, but Mike wouldn't answer. Johnnie climbed down fast and I followed, the bottom rung gave way as I jumped the last three feet to the ground. I caught up with Johnnie in time to hear him call to Mike, "I'm going home. If you tell Mom, I'll kick your ass."

Johnnie turned, and passed me on the narrow path in the woods. I decided to hang out with Mike, who perked up with the attention. We reached the creek as the sun waned. Shadows grew long like the trees, and formed dark patterns on glistening ice. Thinking I might raise Mike's spirits, and feeling cocky having smoked my first cigarette, I eased the toe of my boots out on the ice. Solid.

I walked a few steps out, turned, and slid back to shore. I walked further out, turned, ran, and flew over the slick surface. Mike watched, but would not venture from shore. He called, "I can't swim."

I churned my legs hard to get up speed for one last, long free glide to the center of the frozen stream, and called out, "You don't have to swimmmmm…"

᛭

As my head and shoulders rose back into the crisp air, I heard Mike hollering while he ran scared, "I'll get help."

Stuck and stunned, I imagined little Mike charging through the woods and across the ball diamond, climbing the ridge, slipping and pawing his way up, and finally reaching the crest. Looking up, he would run the long grade of our blacktop street, past the Raymond's, past Paul's house. In my driveway, Pop would be waiting.

Wet and shaking from the cold creek, and thirty feet from shore, panic eased to fear. Fear turned to determination. As I tried a step upstream, my boot dislodged a round stone from the muddy bottom. My thigh cracked a bit of ice on the surface. Not sure I could keep my balance crosswise to the current, I trudged again, upstream, this time angling toward shore. Trees on the bank seemed closer, but the ice grew thicker, and even more slippery from water splashed on the surface. Afraid to climb, as I would surely slip, and be swept under.

Before I saw the rope, my brother's red hair appeared through the bushes. I knew then I would not drown. Dennis, the only one home, had jumped on my bike, and flown down the path to the ball field. He wrapped a rope around a tree, and tossed the other end to me, "Tie it around your waist."

As Dennis pulled, I slid across the slippery surface, and finally grabbed a root protruding from the bank. He cradled me under both arms and yanked, "What the hell were you doing?"

He led me through the woods. My legs wobbled, but as I walked, feeling returned, and the cold became bearable.

When we reached the clearing, I saw the bike propped up against the chicken wire backstop. Shivering, I climbed up on the handlebars while my brother pedaled the two-track up the ridge, then up the blacktop street to our concrete drive.

In his calm, commanding voice, Dennis ordered, "Get those clothes off, I'll run a lukewarm tub. You could get frostbite."

I thought I would never stop shaking. "Hot water," I called.

Dennis struggled to pull my soaked jeans over my foot. His frown told me no.

When Pop came home from work, he nearly slipped on a puddle near the front door, and asked what I was doing in my "pj's?"

"Dennis saved my life," I replied.

I told most of the story, though my adventure seemed less remarkable, and lost luster in the telling.

My big brother looked on with his knowing, witty smile.

LA CUCARACHA

Paul's house had a double garage and a wide L-shaped driveway. Up against the white brick, his dad mounted a basketball hoop on a backboard, painted black. The concrete, laid in cut sections, marked out a perfect square. After the World Series, but before the first snowfall, the neighborhood gang gathered at Paul's, the best basketball court around.

The garage doors had to be closed so a wayward ball evaded the three-cylinder Saab parked inside. Only Paul's dad drove the Saab, the most exotic car in the neighborhood. His mom would watch out the window, especially when Paul's twerpy little brother Steven came out. "Never call him Stevie," she instructed. We had to let him play.

Paul's mom treated me like one of their family. She gave me a hug and tucked me in on Friday nights when I slept over. She let Paul and me stay up to watch "The Twilight Zone." Rod Serling's eerie narrative voice still echoes through black and white scenes in my mind. She even let me sleep in Steven's twin bed. Steven had to sleep in the guest bedroom. Paul's dad didn't like me displacing his younger son, and though Mr. Chandler kept his comments to himself, I saw his gruff look. As soon as the lights went out, Paul and I talked back and forth across the dark, until growing bored, we shook our synthetic blankets, and static sparks flickered in the dark.

At my hankering, Pop agreed to mount a hoop on our garage. We painted the backboard brown to blend in with the reddish-beige bricks. Dennis had joined a fraternity at Delaware, and moved into the "Kappa Alpha House." Pop had married the housekeeper, Grace, for company, and so someone was there to meet me when I came home from school. Grace's kisses were even sloppier than Grandma's.

Only Grace and I were around to help Pop bolt the backboard into the brick façade above the garage. Pop wore an old pair of slacks from a worn out wool suit, and a good white dress shirt, sleeves folded at the wrist. I knew the slacks were old because one of the belt loops in back had broken loose, and stuck out like a tail.

Pop climbed up the ladder, while grasping the painted plywood with a hand on each edge, and slid the wood up the ladder rails as he stepped. Grace hung out a window just above the garage to help hold the backboard. With my foot bracing the ladder, I noticed Paul standing on the sidewalk, and smiling while he watched the evolution.

When the hoop reached the ten foot mark, Pop fully extended his arms, stretched his legs, and raised the backboard so that Grace could hold it in place. A moment before her hands touched the plywood, Pop's pants dropped to his ankles. He stood on the ladder, holding the backboard high above his head, with his boxer shorts exposed to the neighborhood.

Paul, hands swinging above his head, sang "La Cucaracha." He danced, snapped his fingers, and strolled down the sidewalk as if on stage at Radio City Music Hall.

Pop survived the embarrassment, bolted the backboard up, and felt a lot better after several evening highballs. The gang came and played at my new court for the next few days. We had some good games, but we only had a single car driveway, and gradually, for the bigger games, more than two on two, we played at Paul's house.

The next Saturday at Paul's, we had four on a side going. I drove in hard for a layup and missed. We called our own, and I called, "foul."

Paul retorted, "No way."

I lowered my shoulder and charged, and with a clean tackle, took him to the ground. Paul shoved me off. We both jumped to our feet, and started boxing with bare fists. I caught him good, bloodying his nose. Mr. Chandler rushed out the side door, yanked me hard away from Paul, and said, "You go on home. Everybody go home. Find a new place to play."

Mrs. Chandler, Paul's mom, watched from the window.

Paul and I had fought often, like brothers do. After a day or so we'd shrug it off and forget it happened. But this time was different. Older and stronger, the time had come for us both to grow up. Mrs. Chandler made sure of that.

Several days passed. I would see Paul from a distance, but we would not acknowledge each other. I passed by Mrs. Chandler out gardening, and she stared, knowingly. I missed Paul, and I missed her.

The gang grew tired of playing hoops at my house. One evening, two weeks after the fight, I finished my homework late, and headed out on my bike to find the guys. I heard shouting and the ball bouncing, two doors down at Paul's court. I parked my bike on the kickstand, walked over to Paul, and sheepishly blurted out, "I'm sorry."

Paul walked me out toward the front lawn. He suddenly looked mature. He had grown older, more serious. "So what about the next time? It's just gonna' happen again."

I took a deep breath and exhaled, pleading, "No, no more."

"Better not. Mom says that has to be the last time."

We shook hands, and the other guys laughed. Mrs. Chandler looked lovingly out the window as Paul and I walked back to the court, alternating dribbles.

◈

The weekend before we moved back to Michigan, I spent Friday night at the Chandler's. Mr. Chandler was out of town on business, so Paul's mom made Sloppy Joes, my favorite.

Paul looked at me and asked, "Who do you love more, your real mother or your step mother?"

Mrs. Chandler hugged me warmly, and answered for me, "His real mother, of course."

I had never thought about it before.

ROYAL OAK

Some houses are happier than others. A fact undeniable, yet often un-spoken.

We moved to a gentle boulevard where old trees overhung the sidewalk. Houses appeared comfortable, each one different, yet each one in place. Two story colonials stood tall and white with understated black trim, and contrasted with wooden ranches and modern brick Capes. Sturdy oaks and red maples softened the lines in Royal Oak, an established, Detroit suburb on the north edge of nice, where Pop brought me to live. Years younger than my siblings who had gone off to college, I had become an only child.

Pop put a lot of money into renovating our sprawling ranch house, with new carpets, a coat of paint, and a den with parquet wooden floors. We used the same old kitchen set though, a bamboo table and chairs, all bound by hemp. Pop never lived in Hawaii, nor ever visited a south sea island. Why bamboo, so exotic? I always wondered, but never asked.

I had my own room, actually a pick of bedrooms, but I took a small one with two doors. One door led to a hallway, the other to the den. I figured out that the den had been added on to the house because a large, outside window, the kind with slatted, translucent glass that opened with a crank, filled the wall that separated my bedroom from the den.

We had moved in mid-winter, during the second term of my sixth grade year, before what would have been my crowning year of little league, my chance to redeem myself, and make the all-stars. We moved in the middle of my time as a king pin in elementary school, because in those days, junior high began in seventh. We moved from a place where everyone knew me, a kid who got all A's in school work, yet something far less in conduct, from a place where I knew everyone.

Pop received a promotion, and became the top comptroller for Chrysler Defense. In Delaware he had built tanks. In Michigan, he built rockets. In 1962, missiles carried nukes. Pop made me proud to be his son. I felt important. Every few months, he brought home a new car on executive lease.

I would see him briefly in the morning. He rose early and donned a fresh, dry-cleaned suit each day, though first, in sharply-pressed pants and an armless tee, he prepared two soft-boiled eggs and buttered toast. He always asked if I wanted an egg, and sometimes I did.

Late in the evening, he returned home, still dressed like his suit hung fresh in the closet. Grace, my step-mother, who used to be our house-keeper, had a highball waiting, and dinner on the stove. Several nights a week, they were off to a bridge tournament. Pop was a Master, he could play with the best of them. Some nights, they went out to eat, and Grace would leave me a T-bone steak, a can of corn, and potato chips. Those were the best nights. I'd pop the corn into a pan, and grill the steak in the oven broiler, set up a TV tray, and watch the Red Wings. And try to be in bed, be asleep, before they came home, so I wouldn't hear when the yelling started. But the rippled glow of light shining through slatted window panes kept me awake.

My new class was overloaded with girls. Only seven other boys, and they already had best friends. In any conversation, I became a third wheel. Come that spring, the little league teams had fulfilled the quota of twelve-year-olds, so I had to play softball, fast-pitch softball, for the church team. The kids on the church team didn't seem to care if I had gotten chubby from too many nights of Vernors' ginger ale and chips in front of the television.

But I cared, and in July, Grace took me to the Doctor, for headaches. The doctor saw through me, and suggested a diet, a thousand calories a day. After a few days with no chips, I saw through myself, and got with the program. I mowed our one acre lawn with a push mower twice a week. I trimmed the bushes. I rode my bike. Everywhere. To new places, down new streets. I flew on my single gear Schwinn like a lone Blue Angel.

The last week of summer, before Junior High, I overheard a couple of the guys from school challenging each other to a bike race. The rules were simple, a quarter mile sprint from the ball field across from the elementary school to the next cross street. Both of these guys had played little league, and had snickered about me playing softball. They both had new ten-speeds, and bragged about which was faster. Both started out in low gear, and got a quick lead before my leg muscles kicked in. I will always treasure the look on their faces when I beat them by fifty yards.

&

I entered Junior High the year the Beatles shook their mops on the Ed Sullivan Show. The girls bought records, forty-fives. Such simplistic lyrics, and basic three chord rhythms, but the band was greater than four individuals. Girls swooned, fell all over the stage, and were carted away when coming too close to these god-like figures.

I had played trumpet in the school band since fourth grade, and liked the swing of show tunes, and New Orleans jazz. When I felt down and out, I'd grab my horn, and alone in my room, imagine I was Louis Armstrong, while working out the rhythm to "Bye-Bye Birdie." I appreciated all sorts of music, and understood that the most basic peace of mind can be felt within the vibration of a single note.

My Schwinn was fast, but not cool, so I took off the wheels, and spray-painted over the basic black with metallic green and blue, like a rock poster from San Francisco I must have seen in my dreams. Pop shook his head.

Each day, until the snow set in, I rode my bike the mile and a half across town to Jane Addams Junior High. The few guys I had known from elementary went to another school. I joined the band, and tried out for football, for three days. Lots of running, and old guys yelling like banshees. Organization ruined football. Coaches ruined football. Carefree autumn days of passing the ball with my real buddies back in Newark, days of grass-stained jeans from tackle without pads, had disappeared. When I told Pop I quit, he said, "I don't blame you. But you know, if you don't play now, you probably won't play in high school."

Besides band, I was in the advanced placement classes, and quickly identified the popular girls, the cute ones. I also recognized the tough guys, greasers, guys who even in seventh grade, wore black, pointed-toe shoes with cleats. Slicked back, black-haired guys, not blond like me, guys with brass knuckles and switch blades, guys who always wanted to fight. I seemed to draw their attention.

I switched to French horn, and moved from third chair to first, where the melody was more interesting. We had to buy white-duck pants for marching, and the concerts. I got stuck trying to figure out why white pants were named for ducks.

A skinny kid named Henry played first chair trumpet. In the early fall, he invited me over. His house was on the way home. Henry liked the Beatles, and had all their record albums, 33 rpm, and we listened down in his basement, and he swooned something like the girls. He made me nervous.

I met another guy from band, Bruce, who was on the swim team. His dad was rich, and all the popular girls liked him. But they didn't know, and I never told, about the time we were wrestling in his basement, and his wrestling became grappling, and his hips started moving, and he tried to kiss me. I shook away and ran to the bathroom and locked the door. I didn't see Bruce much after that, but one day in school, as he walked down the hall with one of the popular girls, he made a point of commenting to me, "I like your kind of fun now."

The Friday before Thanksgiving, our first junior high dance was scheduled. But around noon, the principal announced over the loudspeaker that the dance was cancelled, and school was letting out early. President Kennedy had been shot. I watched the convertible in black and white, over and over, and struggled with feelings of guilt, because I really wanted to go to the dance.

Thanksgiving morning came along. I watched "Miracle on 34th Street" and the parades while lying on the couch in the den, until time came to go to Aunt Emily's for dinner. My mother's older sister lived in a big old house in Birmingham, a swanky suburb a few miles north of Royal Oak. Uncle Joe worked for the newspaper, the Free Press, and reminded me of Jimmy Durante. He was bald, and had the same sort of nose. My older cousins would be there, and the atmosphere would be lively and fun. The adults would drink, and no one would say anything about Grace being there, and no one would say anything about Sally Jane, my mother, not being there.

I found lots of places to hide at Aunt Em's house, to be alone, and listen. Places where I thought I might catch a glimpse of my mother hidden in the words floating through the woodwork. Pop must have felt her too. And Grace. She must have felt out of place, a replacement, a substitute for a star.

We left early. Pop was loaded, and lapsed in and out of sleep while Grace drove home. What started it this time? Pop wanted to go back out, find a drink somewhere. Grace took the keys. His eyes flared like an enraged horse's nostrils. He picked up a bamboo chair, raised it high over his head, and smashed the chair to pieces on the floor. Grace threw the keys at him, and he charged her, fists raised.

I felt a surge of confidence, and pangs of responsibility. No longer the husky, spoiled kid, and Pop had turned soft from years behind a desk. I stepped in his path, grabbed both his wrists, and held his arms. Grace found the keys, and while I held on, ran out the door. Pop broke one hand free, and raised it as if to cuff my head.

We stood in time, my father and I. Our eyes met. Mine, grown strong yet pleading. His, still wild but softening. We both heard the car start outside. I loosened my grip, and Pop dropped his hand. What would my mother have said?

I ran out the front door and down the dark sidewalk under overhanging hardwood trees. I ran and ran and ran. At the end of the street across from the ball field, a wooded area separated houses from the road. I tucked myself in beneath a bush, and held my knees with my arms, and realizing I had no coat, felt the cold November air creep into my bones.

Will I sleep here? Can I somehow call Aunt Em? A car moved on the street. Grace. I ran from my hiding place and flagged her down. She looked at me with fear in her eyes, but reluctantly opened the door.

We went to the movies. "Gypsy Rose Lee" was a little risqué for me, not quite thirteen, but I had always been given some latitude with regard to age. I didn't even notice the parts where Gypsy performed her burlesque act. I knew the theatre was like my hiding spot in the woods, temporary, but warmer.

Grace dropped me off back at the house where Pop slept on the couch in front of a blaring television. She said goodnight from the driver's window, and drove east, to an aunt back in Pennsylvania.

I switched off the television, crept into my little room with two doors, and tried to sleep, bothered by the glare from the slatted window, and incessant feedback running through my head. Maybe if I can just sleep, the madness will go away.

PELOT

I don't know if he died yesterday or last year. I heard he died peacefully, in his sleep.

The first day of school in 64', eighth grade, and we were both new kids, ostracized in a small Ohio town. Most had lived there, together since kindergarten, so we were the new guys, and both in the advanced classes. Sure, we liked football, but not like these guys. In Ohio, football was religion. Pelot and I were agnostic.

He was sort of scrawny, and he followed me around a lot. He would pop up without warning, his face a little too large for his body, and he harbored the quickest wit I will ever know. Pelot knew what I was thinking before I did.

His mom was an alcoholic and divorced. Not too common back then. His old man put up with him, but the new wife didn't like him. Pelot spent a lot of time at our place, a habit that would last for years.

We turned fourteen, and learned to play the guitar together. Pelot would strut around like Mic, while I sat quietly, and listened to soft sounds emanating from my round, wooden flat top. We were not identical peas, but thrust together in a pod, nonetheless.

We took first and second in the eighth grade writing contest. Mine was first, "I'll Try Again," about a young, lonely, and misunderstood boy who wanted to run away but was unable to find the nerve. Pelot wrote a science fiction story about spaceships, and aliens who played the guitar. I spent the ten dollar prize on picks and a capo, so I could work out the chords on a Beach Boys song he already knew.

We made it together through eighth grade. Then I found a girlfriend, and he kept hanging around. She had a friend and Pelot was sort of stuck. The friend had a big nose, more a beak, but then so did Pelot.

August was hot on the Ohio suburban plains. Pelot stopped by my house. My step mom had returned home from one of her frequent trips away to visit her aunt. She didn't like Pelot much. He walked in the kitchen, and talked football practice starting soon, "You playing?"

I had bagged out of football in eighth grade. I made the excuse to those who asked that I had a hernia operation when I was twelve, and couldn't play, my parents wouldn't let me. In truth, I was scared, and felt like the fat guy in the corner who couldn't run wind sprints.

And here was Pelot, skinny, scrawny, yet unafraid to run with the big guys. "Practice starts tomorrow."

My step mom looked at me, "Are you going to play?"

Caught.

The hernia was not a problem, though I did have the operation when I was twelve. She knew that but didn't let on. Pelot looked at me with a knowing glance, without words, saying, you can play!

And I did.

One of the best decisions I had made in my short life to that point. But I had not made the decision, Pelot made it for me.

I ended up starting at linebacker, and the team went undefeated. Pelot never got in a game. But every day he picked me up, made me laugh, and told me, "Man, you're good." I finally began to believe him.

&

I heard Pelot had passed, and part of me died, too, though I hadn't talked to him in twenty years.

CHAPTER TWO

WANDERING

ODE TO PETE

He was of my father's generation
But not of my father.
He sang for my father,
songs my father never knew.
I knew the songs. I sang the songs.
I wore Levi pants and chambray shirts.
I worked in sawmills and drove trucks,
and planted corn and combined corn from the ear,
and sang his songs of working men.

I traveled his empty highways
and sailed with brothers on the deep blue sea.
And, like my father who had worked his way
up from the field, yet never knew the songs,
worked my way up, never forgetting the songs.
I fought for the flowers,
wondered "where they've gone,"
wondered why
Woody left too young,
a victim of the hard road.

But Pete carried on
and taught Bobby, and Joan,
Arlo followed along.
Many of us listened well to the message.
The boundless, beautiful message,
rings out still, hate only hate.

A smiling face, a frailing banjo,
the golden valley.
And like Tom Joad,
Pete will never die.

LEAVING ALBION

Weaving my Royal Enfield through dark curves over two lane black-top, I wondered at how easily friends weave in and out of this life, like threads in a bright tapestry hanging on the walls of my mind. I took a bike trip, but more, a venture in time travel, where faces unseen for forty years came alive, and smiled at me in vivid color.

❧

Two years after the Detroit riots, caped graduates waited in alphabetical order, behind velvet curtains draped from the orbital ceiling heights of the Masonic Auditorium. A moment before Principal Disbrow called me onto the stage, a gusher of crimson burst forth from my nose. A kid next to me in line, whom I hardly knew, reluctantly handed me his white hand-kerchief. I dabbed, and dizzy, climbed the three steps up to the platform, and walked across a never-ending stage. I shook with my right hand, and gathered my diploma with my left, still cupping a balled, borrowed cloth. Old Man Disbrow stared silently. A falling drop of blood missed the sheepskin, formed into a perfectly round spot, and stained the gold cord hung around my neck.

Something looked different in her eyes. Uneasy, and fidgeting, she stood, shapely, in the parking lot behind Dominico's Italian Restaurant. Perfectly proportioned curves drew me to Janice. Her tanned, gently mus-cled legs beckoned beneath the blue sundress she had worn below her gown. She wanted marriage, a child, or a child and marriage, the order of things didn't seem to matter. I wanted to see the world.

Janice pleaded, "Everybody's going out to Billy's cabin later, Jimmie Mac, and Bob White. This is the biggest night of our lives, graduation night, I want to go."

"I have to work early tomorrow." I had to get up at six the next morn-ing to make the lumberyard. Aunt Emily had pulled strings to get me a good summer job unloading boxcars of lumber coming in by rail from the northern forests. The yard paid $3.65 an hour as long as I joined the Teamsters' Union. Along with my Scholarship, the money I earned would cover my first year's tuition, room, and board at Albion College.

I winced, and watched Janice walk away, like a model down a runway.

Every twenty miles, I looked for a shade tree along the highway, a place to stretch, and check my crumpled, fold out map. My single cylinder Enfield vibrated wildly, and thumped with each revolution. When nature called, I stopped near a bridge over a woodsy little creek. I peeled off my helmet and jacket for relief from the hot sun. Bug stains accumulated on the black leather. I walked into the woods bordering the stream bottom, unzipped my jeans, and to my surprise, felt nothing. My pecker had gone numb.

I needed to find a place to stay before darkness fell. Checking the map, I found a little town thirty miles down the road. A little town called Albion.

The arrival of an unsigned letter advising that my scholarship had not been renewed failed to surprise me. Writers of letters, protectors of the realm of conformity, wielded power, hid in darkness, invisible behind mahogany paneled walls, and never revealed their names. I had made good grades, nothing less than a 'B', but a string of external events paralleled a growing restlessness in my mind.

My stepmother died that February, after fighting breast cancer for several years. She died the same way my mother had, slowly, and painfully, while my father watched, again.

I went home for the funereal. Janice stopped by the house later. In a small bedroom off the kitchen, my uncertain grief gave way to desire. She dressed quickly. Her lovely heels pounded heavy on the kitchen floor, as she left for good.

Only baseball took me back to finish my second semester at Albion.

I had trouble seeing the ball while taking batting practice in a cage inside the dark gym. My eyes worked better in sunlight. Matt Kramer, a senior Captain, threw junk. He seemed outwardly friendly, but I sensed some arrogant resentment. I hadn't played football like they were expecting, and refused to join Matt's jock fraternity. Hell, I thought my academic scholarship had been awarded for academics. Crouching in the cage, my knee ached from a cross-body block thrown in my last high school football game. A seasoned pitcher, Matt played with my head, and was happy to report to the coach that I couldn't hit him.

Finally, on a cool early spring day, practice moved outdoors. I shagged fly balls with several other outfielders under the watchful eyes of our grizzly old coach, Morley Fraser, who, after a few warm-up tosses called out, "Let's see your arms."

Playing the fungo perfectly, I made the catch high on my left side, effortlessly transferred the ball to my right hand, took one stride on my left leg, and let the horsehide fly. The hardball smacked into the second basemen's glove precisely where he had positioned himself to make a tag. He pulled off his glove and shook his hand to relieve the sting.

Fraser smirked, and yelled, "Go work out with the pitchers."

&

My bad knee ached as I rode down College Avenue past grass lawns without weeds, and stately red brick halls. The women's dorm was still there, forty years later, with nurtured ivy neatly framing the white window trim. I slowed to let two young, shapely coeds cross the street. Carefree, with long hair flowing in the slight breeze, they surrendered no acknowledgement to an old, silver-haired guy on a motorcycle.

&

In the spring of 1970, even privileged young people had to protest something. We took our futile stand at the women's dorm. I made the naïve mistake of believing that Birmingham debutantes really wanted their midnight curfew lifted. Stubborn and idealistic, I stayed ensconced on a comfortable couch, occupying the living room and reception area where young women were called to receive their male guests; where I had been received when Janice visited once, in the fall, and we ended up in the Shady Grove Motel.

Warnings came, "There will be consequences."

Others filtered out, concerned about what their mothers and fathers might think. Who would pay the bills? Suddenly, I looked around, and I was alone in the spacious hall. Ray Miller, an upper classman I knew from home, walked in. Ray, also on scholarship, had volunteered to talk to me. "The President said he'll kick you out if you don't leave here now."

As I walked out, I knew that I would be leaving Albion anyway. Seeking something that mattered, I joined an environmental group called SEE, Students for an Ecological Environment. Across the country, committed souls smelled fresh spring air, dreamed of seeing streams flow clean, and prepared for the first Earth Day. SEE did not appear on the administration's list of approved extra-curricular activities. I began to understand that the straight and narrow path through Albion's courtyards could no longer hold me.

Then, on May fourth, they finally did it. They killed four kids just like me at Kent State.

Classes, grades, and even baseball no longer mattered. I stuck out my thumb looking for a ride east toward the Pennsylvania Turnpike and Washington D.C. Nearly a million of us made the trip, travelling by bus or Volkswagen. I slept, riding through dark and hilly Allegheny curves in a converted delivery van.

The next night I slept on the marble steps of the Lincoln Memorial. Rumors spread like whispers, "Nixon was here, he actually talked to us."

Rumors, like dreams we could stop the war.

SIOUX FALLS

He turned the Volkswagen bug off the two lane highway onto a narrow dirt track that led down to a creek. A small, steel sign, pockmarked with bird shot read, "Sioux Falls."

The puppies needed water. The car's cracked, air-cooled engine block shuddered in ninety-five degree heat. A cramped party of five, the woman-child, two young guys, and the dogs, had driven through the night to avoid the summer sun, and in the dark recesses of the crowded car, to avoid each other.

Fanny slept wedged beneath the driver's seat under his legs like a stuffed bear. She looked up with trusting eyes as he lifted her ball of four week old fur. She stumbled on unsure legs, but happily followed him down a dirt path toward the oasis.

The river ran in a sparse trickle, like a spilled bucket, and cut a miniature canyon through a dry, sandy bottom. Black, basswood branches lay broken, and strewn in clusters connected by prairie grasses that had been washed down by spring floods. Fanny splashed in the cool water while he stretched in the shade.

❧

The girl reached into the back seat for the cooler, and disturbed Ganga, a young Rhodesian ridgeback splayed across the other man's lap. She used the last of the peanut butter on three slices of canned brown bread. A spoonful of strawberry jelly remained in the jar. The trip was winding down.

Coming in from Montana, she had struggled, and slept in fitful spurts. Her neck ached from the awkward, twisted angle of her head against the window glass, through which she saw her own eyes each time she woke. In her tired reflections, she thought she glimpsed the truth. The past two months had flown by like barn swallows, dipping and diving through the night, searching for a nest.

Images imprinted in her mind: a white room; slurping stolen watermelon in a small Indiana town; a wide sandy beach near Corpus Christi, where the sun scorched his skin; five dollars wasted on the young Mexican boy who showed them the sights of Metamora; a native shaman selling desert dreams; and blueberry ice cream at a desert wayside.

They camped fearing grizzlies in Rocky Mountain National Park, and hiked to the summit. Lying on cool grass amidst stones, they stared at the clouds, and saw the beginning of the end.

Speechless from the heat of Death Valley in mid-summer sun, they ran from Los Angeles smog, back to nature, and the grandeur of the ocean along the Pacific Coast Highway. On to San Francisco, bright colors and dirty feet, books, and music on the street, dogs, and Frisbee in the park.

Camping, back down the raw Pacific coast, she searched for her vision, and left him alone alongside a creek in Big Sur.

Replaying each scene in her mind, she reasoned with herself. Since San Francisco, the other man had wedged into their private world, pried them apart, and stolen the joy.

She pulled away silently though her head spun with words. Words that remained unspoken in the crowd of people who squeezed life, like juice from a lime. He had needed a dog, something to divert his attention, while she planned her leaving.

❧

The engine had cooled down. The trip had entered a denouement, the way that Altamont had killed the dream. He knew it was over, and turned his head into the breeze.

He hoped the cracked block would last the final six-hundred miles, long enough to carry Fanny home, to Michigan.

A black and white steel sign, pockmarked with bird shot, faded away, and became a blemish on the rear-view mirror.

LADY GODIVA

A door entered the apartment above from a bedroom in the addition below. Heather would visit from time to time.

Loneliness pervades a young man's life with tentacles that reach like nerve endings into the very tips of his fingers. The feeling had begun before I left my buddies and college to travel through Europe. I was driven to live independent of others, who would only let me down. Yet, I waited endless hours for her, just for some knowledge of the outside world, and a little human company.

Fanny Tuesday, my dog and companion, lived with my Aunt at the farm while I travelled, but never failed to greet my return with joy. Mornings, Fanny and I took long walks in the fallow fields of the section of land that my family owned. One time, I returned from a walk, and looking down, noticed that my shoes, socks, and jeans below the knee, had become soaked with dew.

Pelot, who visited the farm once or twice, happened to be waiting at the house when I returned, and chuckled aloud, "Getting your feet wet?"

Happy to never take myself too seriously, I understood that no real farmer would walk miles through wet grass when there was work to be done.

❧

Heather often took me riding horseback along slow trails to the Black River. Small flat farm fields, still surrounded by windbreaks, gave way to the broad river valley that dropped two hundred feet to fertile, forested bottomland. The windbreaks, where pheasant and grouse and other game lived, are gone now from Michigan. Gone to the factory farms, where earth movers pile mountains of beets for Pioneer Brand Sugar alongside paved country highways. Gone to developments of identical mini-mansions, gone to a place where a mere acre of land makes a country boy. Gone are fields on the high ridge where we rested, where our whole world, our unknown future, lay ahead in endless possibilities.

The first time, I rode Annie, Heather's gentle appaloosa mare. We left Booger, a big strong gelding who thought he was a stallion, alone in the pasture. Heather rode Joe, a trusty old gelding who got along with every-one. I had ridden some, but it took living close to the horses, close to the earth's diurnal clock, to begin to understand horses as intelligent beings, as steady friends, who could be counted upon in a pinch.

A winding trail led to the river bottoms. We followed the river south to an old gravel pit, where we stopped to water the horses. On warm, windless days, I climbed the etched rock wall to show-off with a dive into an unkempt pool.

◌

Heather wanted to go on a real date, to Canada, where the drinking age was eighteen. She had a boyfriend, a Sergeant, a long way away, serving in Vietnam. We crossed the St. Clair River over the Blue Water Bridge at Sarnia. The same bridge where Pop had run booze during Prohibition to earn his way through college. The bridge now has two spans to handle the traffic of shoppers who take advantage of the currency exchange. And for the trucks that haul Toronto's garbage into Michigan. It makes so little sense to bury trash in a state built on sand, with aquifers running beneath the Great Lakes. Another windbreak lost to progress.

Vodka and Squirt were easy to drink, and we danced to a bad rock and roll band. The ride home was a blur in my borrowed, black barracuda. She looked at me from the passenger seat, "that was fast." I had enough patriotism not to want to try to steal a soldier's girl.

◌

Heather brought girlfriends out to the farm. On sunny days, they would skip classes at the junior college to go riding. Joanie, a game brunette, liked to hang around the farmhouse and drink beer or smoke a joint.

Gail had an air of classic beauty, an almost French quality. She was the first to marry, a local kid, a high school sweetheart, but it didn't last.

Julie, tall, thin and striking, also went with a high school sweetheart. When she decided to leave, he feigned suicide, with a twenty-two rifle aimed at his chest. He suffered a glancing flesh wound. She left anyway.

Glenda, Heather's closest friend, was an artist frustrated by junior college teachers who couldn't paint a wall. She often stayed nights at the farm when things at home went bad. Her father constantly berated her, and sapped her confidence. Her whole life lay in the creation of beautiful things, yet he forced her to take nursing classes, while she worked two jobs. He refused to pay for her schooling, but never hesitated to borrow money when he needed a loan. Down the road apiece, the old man and I would have words.

The first time I saw Glenda, she rode Booger, bareback. I watched from an upstairs window. White linen curtains gently swayed in the autumn breeze. She rode alone across the pasture toward the barn. Her blackish brown hair, woven in strands like a lover's knot, extended below her waist. She galloped through the field, quickly changed to a trot, reined in just short of the gate, and hopped off, in timeless, fluid motion.

My path came to me in a vision.

She didn't notice me that day at the window, or even much on other sunny days, or on evenings when I strummed my Martin, and sang for the girls.

55' CHEVY

My buddy Pelot and I set out to hitch to San Francisco from the farm in St. Clair County, Michigan, in the early December cold of 1971. Rides were damn hard to come by. Few would dare pick up two long-haired guys, each carrying a guitar, and Fanny, my dog, who trailed behind. We pooled our cash, and came up with less than a hundred bucks, mostly mine.

Just eighty miles down the road, two Ohio State Troopers picked us up off the turnpike ramp, hauled us in to the station in Maumee, and fined us five dollars apiece for vagrancy. A cop behind a counter took our money, "You're free to go."

We walked out into the dark, small town night bantering insults, but elated, "At least they didn't fine the dog."

After walking a block, and seeing no patrol cars, we hitchhiked back to the turnpike. The ticket still resides in my guitar case, and I look at it from time to time, "…did loiter to solicit a ride."

Late evening on the third day, we made Davenport, across the Mississippi River. Cold and tired, we found an all-night café. Bad coffee loaded with sugar and half n' half, and the local gazette had been left strewn on the table. Pelot and I took turns trying to sleep, while the other sipped coffee so we didn't get thrown out. I closed my eyes to nightmare visions of the night before, passing by Joliet Prison, a haunting monolith lurking behind razor fences, backlit by dirty snow.

While Pelot slept, I read the classifieds. "Used 1955 Chevrolet, runs, $50." Sometime after daylight, I stepped up to the counter with the paper, "Is River Street close by?"

The lanky waitress, who put up with us through the night, motioned with her arms, "Two blocks down toward the river, and it's a good thing you have a pretty dog. Here, take this leftover toast for her."

I knocked on the door at the River Street address exactly at eight am. Pelot stood on the lawn, holding Fanny in tow. A middle aged man, unshaven, stood on the porch stoop and pointed to the car, "Yah, runs good. I'm out of work and need the money."

The Chevy started on the first turn of the key. He drove me around the block. I counted out the fifty dollars, and he signed over the title. Taking a chance, he said, "I'll leave the Iowa plates, but get them changed before you leave town."

She was a tank, a big, warm, and wonderful tank. Rusty colored, or maybe baby shit brown with rust lining the panels, the Chevy had a heater but no radio. Pelot got in the passenger side, propped his feet up on the metal dashboard and started bitching, "I'd never buy a car without a radio!"

I scowled back, "Would you rather walk to the West Coast?"

Neither the top of the line Bel-Air, nor the model that car junkies like to soup-up and restore, yet she gave us a basic, fifty-dollar ride when no one else would. I have owned and driven many nice cars in my life. But in that moment of poverty, the Chevy, more than a car, her heater warm as we rambled, protected us within her womb.

I watched jack rabbits dodging in front of the Chevy as I drove through the snowy Wyoming night. More likely the over the counter speed I had swallowed. Cowboys hanging out in a truck stop in Laramie didn't flinch when a tall lanky waitress with a nice smile delivered four cups of coffee using just one arm. She tossed cups across the counter like a Vegas' dealer shuffling cards on a felt table. Years later, I read some of those cowboys killed a college kid in Laramie for sport, just because he wasn't right.

After driving all through the night, morning dawned to the reddish-yellows of the Great Salt Lake. Pelot woke up from time to time, and threw a jab across the wide space of the Chevy's interior, "Still think you're seeing rabbits?"

He took a turn at the wheel, while I stared out the passenger window at miles and miles of seductive, salty-white desert landscape, and searched for hot cars flying over the Bonneville Flats.

A pall filled the air when we passed a green highway sign illuminated with the words "Donner Pass." The next sign warned of fines for crossing the Sierras without tire chains. The balding, black walled tires on the Chevy shook on the grooved pavement. Pelot's eyes grew wider, he warned, "Keep her moving, I don't want to spend the night in Donner Pass."

As if in a dream, the Chevy reached the summit, and began a long glide down toward Sacramento. Thirty-six hours straight from Iowa, before we crossed the Bay Bridge. I hoped the San Andreas Fault wouldn't choose that moment to shift.

Entering San Francisco, like the dawn of a new day, never fails to exhilarate my senses. Lights twinkled like enchanted stars over rolling hills. But when we left the highway, and worked our way down Army Street, the reality of a wet and cold December in the city set in. We pulled up in a blur at my sister's ground floor, two room flat in the Mission. San Francisco had changed.

&

The first time I visited, two summers earlier, the coast was hippies, sun, and smiles, Frisbees in the park, and dogs running free. I got Fanny that summer, a tri-colored little mutt, the runt of the litter by a Samoyed bitch and a shepherd sire. My traveling companion then suggested I needed a dog, and helped me pick Fanny out as a substitute, while she flirted with the black guy who owned the white Samoyed. Even through my young man's jealousy, I saw things would not last.

My brother-in-law Al, the poet, named Fanny after a literary character of ill repute. Fanny was sexy for a dog. Her face was silver and black, and her eyes and ears were shaded a gentle brown. White markings ran through her chest, marked the tip of her tail, and punctuated the shake of her ass.

&

San Francisco had changed, and more than just the weather. The erstwhile Pelot and I rolled into San Francisco on that dreary evening, and parked the Chevy outside my sister's apartment. Jill and Al were out but soon returned, Al stumbling and laughing, talking loud, and making us laugh as he always did, drunk or sober.

We were welcomed with open arms, at first, smoked a joint, and I fell asleep on the water bed, awakened in the morning by Al's arm across my shoulders. Then there was the look on his face when he awoke to my eyes staring back, rather than my sister's. Somehow I'd ended up between them. Not a good start.

My outlook went from bad to worse, and there must have been a hole in my pocket where money fell out. Any cash I had was spent on gas for the Chevy. I took day trips over the Golden Gate to see a wealthy young girl up in Marin, whom I had met in Ireland. She played wonderfully on her parents' grand piano. A neighbor called out to her, mocking, upon seeing the old Chevy with Iowa plates pull up in front of the hedges that hid her cleverly understated cedar home.

I was running out of time even faster than money, and knew my soul couldn't last the winter in San Francisco.

Before Christmas, I went to see the recruiter, thinking I might sail the seven seas. The sharply dressed Chief really didn't understand why someone like me, one semester short of my bachelor's degree would want to enlist, "I can't promise you any training schools."

Determined, I gave him the same self-assured look I gave the doctor when I went for a physical. I was in good shape, and couldn't get my pulse above sixty during the exercise test. The doctor tried to give me another out. Vietnam was still raging. He was "worried" about my heart, or maybe whether my heart was in my decision. "Are you sure you want this?"

Pelot found a job making pizzas, and rented a basement flat off Delores Avenue. The last night before I left, I walked alone in the wee-dark hours through Dolores Park. I sat on a park bench, and stared at the city lights until dawn broke over Oakland. In the morning, Pelot dropped me off at the recruiter's office, "Still time to change your mind."

I boarded the bus that carried me back across the Bay Bridge, through Oakland and Jack London Square, and arrived at boot camp, on a reclaimed island in the Estuary, a place known simply as Alameda. I traded in my corduroys, moccasins, and a woven belt a friend had made for me, and put on woolen blues.

I gave the Chevy to Pelot, though I made him sign for the title. He also took the dog. He found a good home for Fanny, somewhere with a family and kids.

The Chevy quit while I was in boot camp, and Pelot left it on the street, up near Dolores Park.

WIND

Comes and goes, mysterious,
silent.
A screen door slams
wood on wood.
No one came, no one left.
Bang, goes the screen door,
announces the porch guest
invisible
yet familiar.
Sit awhile, my dear friend.
Tell me all you have seen.
Ah, yes,
tis' a wonderful and varied world.
Alas,
must you leave so soon?

CHAPTER THREE

SEMPER PARATIS – "ALWAYS READY"

PART ONE

TO THE BIRTHPLACE OF THE WINDS

The first time I saw her, she rode bareback across the pasture. I watched from the back window upstairs, white linen curtains blew gently in the autumn breeze. Her thick, blackish-brown hair formed in a weave, bounced joyfully, and extended down, below her waist. The bay horse galloped close to the fence, and slid to a stop just short of the gate. In a symmetrical movement, she hopped off.

The farm existed in blue-collar country. Men didn't go to college, play the guitar, or write songs. Men worked construction, worked the family farm, and went off to soldier. Men made money, drank hard, and drove pickup trucks.

I headed west to seek my fortune, to prove myself, and all the while, remembered her crooked, endearing smile, and the way she laughed, straight from her heart.

❧

A year and a half later, I had received orders to the Coast Guard Air Station on Lake St. Clair, a mere thirty miles from the farm. I served as a flight medic on rescue helicopters, and visited the farm whenever I had a couple days off. Nothing much had changed. Heather and Glenda were still there, both attending the junior college. Attending might be non-descriptive. Glenda only went to her art classes, and skipped the academics to play euchre in the student union. Heather mostly worked at odd jobs, and saved money to travel. She wanted to see the world.

I helped Heather deliver a new bicycle to Glenda for her birthday. The bike fit in my VW Squareback. Glenda had moved into town, to a small flat. I had my Martin on my lap, and played an acoustic arrangement I had written, a piece combining some of my classical training with the twang of folk-rock. While we passed a joint around, the girls swayed, and kept rhythm with the beat. When I eased into a new, unwritten end to the song, Glenda, with her long, dark braid hanging below her waist, picked up her woolen Indian blanket, eased down next to me, and laid the blanket across our joined legs.

On my days off, we spent carefree, summer afternoons. Heather's boyfriend had returned from 'Nam, but things weren't working out. The war changed folks.

Heather bustled with electric energy, and knew everyone within a hundred mile radius of the farm. The three of us took a weekend trip to the beaches by Port Austin to visit a college friend. And on a morning not long after, Heather's mother poured a shot of Canadian whisky in my coffee, looked me in the eyes, and said, "You know, a man takes two girls off overnight, he better marry one of them."

⋉

The Commanding Officer, USCG Officer Candidate School Yorktown, Virginia, read my orders aloud, "Ensign Thomas F. Conlan shall report for duty aboard the United States Coast Guard Cutter Ironwood, homeport, Adak, Alaska. Meet the cutter in Seattle, Washington no later than the 9th of July, 1975."

Fear had followed surprise, and both battled my natural sense of optimism, and my adventurous spirit. I thought about my young wife waiting back in Michigan, and the pending birth of our first child, just two weeks away. My anxiety increased as I recalled listening in on the women's kitchen conversations at Christmastime, "the first baby is often overdue."

I had received a seagoing billet, an honor for a "Mustang," the colloquial term for an officer who came up through the ranks. I would need the spirit of a wild mustang in the years to come.

Adak, a remote island, lies over a thousand miles west of mainland Alaska, where the warm Japanese current meets the cold of the Arctic Ocean and Bering Sea. The native Aleut Indians know Adak as "The Birthplace of the Winds."

⋉

Glenda and I married in September, 1973, after mere weeks together. Our honeymoon followed a year later. We drove my green Dodge step-side pickup from Michigan, bound for Nova Scotia, and camped along the way. Glenda cooked brown rice, scallions, and golden raisins on a two-burner Coleman stove propped on the tailgate. Her green eyes sparkled, and her thick, bay-brown hair still hung in a braid below her waist. Somewhere up in the woods of Maine, she had gorged on too many wild blueberries, bought on the honor system with two dollars in quarters left on a lonely card table. She paid dearly, and later wondered, "I can't figure out what made me sick."

We pitched a tent near a cliff overlooking the Bay of Fundy, which swirled over rocks forty feet below. Around midnight, I awoke to the sound of lapping water nearby, and opened the tent flap to see the surging ocean, which had risen to the top of the cliff at peak flood tide. I turned, and slept enveloped in the relaxing sound of water.

On the morning's ebb tide, we walked the beach, and felt salt water rush to bury our feet in the sand. She gathered mollusks, and dried the colorful shells. She was brilliant, an artist, a painter, a potter, always consumed with the project, the moment, at hand. She lived completely in the present. So unlike me, ever a wandering dreamer, who admired her walk through life with such focus, her surety in each following footstep.

On a hauntingly beautiful afternoon, Glenda and I returned from Nova Scotia to our three-room cabin in Anchor Bay, a village on the shores of Lake St. Clair. The cabin was really a seasonal rental, more of a fishing camp for weekenders, but Glenda convinced the owners up in the main house to let us stay year round. The rent was one hundred twenty-five dollars a month, quite a stretch on my 2nd Class Petty officer pay.

On a rare day off in late September, the sun shone warm, and reflected off the lake. Her green eyes warned of the consequences. My life would be forever changed.

Glenda and I tried to enjoy the Christmas holidays in our pine-paneled cabin under the dark, looming cloud of a six month separation for OCS. We held each other tight throughout a weekend train trip to Toronto, a Christmas present to ourselves. The baby grew inside.

⊱

I returned home in time for Glenda's final Doctor's visit prior to her June

15th due date. Her birth canal was too small, the baby might not fit. We attended the last two Lamaze classes together, and hoped time would solve the problem. But time grew short. "For the health of the baby and the mother," the doctor decided, "we need to deliver by Caesarian section if nothing happens before the 28th." My young wife's eyes revealed her innocence and fear. Outwardly, I remained unfazed, while inside I churned.

I experienced an epiphany when Elsa Marie entered this world. The awesome, essential nature of manhood, of complete responsibility for a woman and a child, was revealed. We named her Elsa, for the wisdom and free spirit of the female lion we admired in the story "Born Free". Marie was for the perfect, innocent Mary, also the name of her birth hospital. Blond and beautiful, loyal and caring, yet strong and independent, Elsa would grow to embody both names.

Holding my daughter for the first time, I understood the inherent goodness of the world. Glenda grew up in an instant, moving from the freedom of childhood in the late Sixties to an innate knowing of motherhood. She held our child nestled naturally in her arms, and I could only look on, a loving bystander to the bonding of mother and daughter.

◌⋌

The letter notifying me of acceptance to Officer Candidate School had arrived the previous autumn, and blew in like an Alberta Clipper wings across Lake Superior. The Coast Guard wanted me, and wanted an answer. The devil had come calling with a deal, a once in a lifetime opportunity, and only a chunk of my soul was required in payment.

OCS was a ticket to success in the straight and narrow world I had always questioned. I admired anti-social heroes, the ones who skirted the edge of the law and prevailed. My lingering childhood favorites included the Lone Ranger, pure good behind a mask, Robin Hood, a workingman's hero, and Ty Cobb, hated by his peers, but he played ball like I had, for keeps, spikes up and get out of my way if you can't take it. My evolution through the late sixties drew me to more cerebral idols. I was inspired by the Dylans, Bob and Thomas, and read all of Twain and Dickens. Whitman instructed me to act upon my conscience, while I became lost in thought reading Emerson's Essays. Al Masarik, my brother-in-law and a talented, struggling, San Francisco poet, had opened my mind to Bukowski, Henry Miller, Ginsberg, Hesse, and Brautigan. Vonnegut taught me to laugh and think, at the same time. I remained a skeptic, and a doubting patriot.

I found myself torn between the promise of success, which would provide security for my growing family, and the risk I thrived upon. My conscience questioned the compromise. But I have always been a traveller, driven to discover an existence beyond the world I know.

In the end, I rationalized my decision, as all men do, and accepted the orders to OCS. I gained security for my family, and a sense of adventure prevailed over any real or imagined pangs of conscience. Hell, I was being paid to go to Alaska.

॰ᴺ

My sense of guilt evaporated in the excitement of the open road. I said my goodbyes at the hospital, and made the twenty-four hundred mile drive to San Francisco in three days and two nights. I caught a few hours rest in my sleeping bag on the bed of the pickup, when my eyes began to close, somewhere in the high desert of Wyoming.

I spent the Fourth of July with Heather and her new husband, Pat, in their San Francisco apartment. Early the next day, we went to the ballpark in Oakland, where Ronny Kirkwood, an old teammate I caught in summer ball, was pitching for the visiting Angels. From across the first row box seat, I saluted, "You made it, huh?"

He was the same old Ronny, grinning, never condescending, though he could throw a ninety-five mile-per-hour fastball. "Yah," he smiled sheepishly. We talked like the old days, and he genuinely seemed more interested in my trip to Alaska than talking about how he led the American League in Earned Run Average.

Wondering whether I could have made the big leagues if I had given it a real shot, I turned the pickup north for a two-day trip to Seattle, the Cutter *Ironwood*, and my future.

In Seattle, I dropped my truck at the Navy terminal for transport to Adak, Alaska, and took a cab to the docks. *Ironwood* was moored to the pier for dockside maintenance.

Glenn Young, second in command, welcomed me aboard, "The Old Man, Captain Black, flew back to New England to visit family. Hey, I see you have a Martin. What do you play?"

"Kind of hard to categorize my style."

"Stow your gear in the forward starboard stateroom, let's see what you've got."

I threw my duffel on the upper rack, and unbuckled my hard shell case. The smell of wood oil and brass strings melded with the hibernating, purple velvet liner.

I thought about my one brief flirtation with desertion, back in Corps School in Great Lakes, Illinois. Pelot, an old buddy, came to "break me out." We had driven through the night in my old VW bug, before the wine wore off, and I dropped him at a bus station in Gary, and returned. A kid with the locker next to mine had remarked, "I didn't think you were coming back, your guitar was gone." I had missed morning muster, and got away with a week's restriction to the base.

"Damn, finally another musician," Young said. " I wish I wasn't leaving now. Show me how you do that, without a pick?"

"I just use the nail on my first finger to strum, and pick with the other three, base with my thumb."

"There's a bar in town called *The Inside Passage*. Some great bluegrass. Let's go."

Over a beer, watching closely, and listening to a good looking woman fiddler exercise her bow on "Orange Blossom Special," I learned that the Cutter would remain dockside for several more weeks, to outfit for the trip home to Alaska.

"Hey, you should sit in," Young suggested.

A pain cut into my side when I realized months might pass before I would see my wife and daughter again. The fiddle sounded like a train starting down some lonely stretch of tracks, "Let's just have another round," I replied.

❧

The Cutter *Ironwood* was built in 1944, one of 36 Seagoing Buoy Tenders assigned to the Navy during World War II, for use in mine-sweeping, and landing support efforts. The ship had been designed with a ten-year life expectancy, but the seaworthiness of the tender proved too durable for the service to ignore. The last of the class, a sister ship of *Ironwood*, was decommissioned in 2006, after more than sixty years afloat.

In late 1974, *Ironwood* had been overhauled, and received new engines at the Coast Guard Shipyard in Curtis Bay, Maryland. Captain Black, Lieutenant Young, and the crew had sailed her on a shakedown cruise through the Panama Canal to Seattle for maintenance before she headed north to Alaska, where shipyards were scarce.

❧

"Why did they send us a fucking Corpsman?" Stubbs spouted, half at me, but his eyes stared at the XO who had just introduced us. "Why not a Quartermaster, or at least a Boatswain's Mate? Jesus, a pecker-checker," he turned away scowling.

"Don't mind him, he'll grow on you," Young commented, while he loaded his gear into his Bronco, and waved goodbye.

Days passed slowly while I learned the book side of my new job, and my dockside duties as both Communications, and Commissary Officer. A new XO, Jim Harrison, short in stature and built like a bowling ball, reported aboard. Jim hailed from San Francisco. We hit it off right away, and learned the intricacies of *Ironwood* together. Jim's first supply order included new sweatshirts for the crew, international orange. When the sweatshirts arrived, he tried one on for size. A brash seaman yelled out from below decks, "It's the Great Pumpkin." Jim had a new nickname.

I called home from the pay phone on the dock in Seattle. "As soon as the Doctor says it's OK, I'll have you on a plane. The government will pay for it. You can stay with Heather in San Francisco for a couple weeks, and then fly north."

Guilt returned, along with a profound concern for mother and newborn. Had the timing of my orders to report to the ship been a factor in the Doctor's decision? I never asked, and will never know.

❧

The morale onboard any ship is largely a result of the quality of meals. Good food breaks up the routine. I observed, not saying much, while ordering basic food stores for the trip to Adak.

"Hey boss" called our salty cook, his white shirt stained from breakfast, "we need lots of ground beef. Can't get it up there. This crew lives on my shit-on-a-shingle."

I had a two-man stateroom to myself. A steel shell, eight feet square, held two built-in desk/closet combinations, two government issue chairs, and two steel bunks mounted on the interior bulkhead. Each bunk was padded with a three inch mattress. I took the lower "rack," but knew I would have to give it up when my bunk mate arrived. An Academy grad, Bob Papp's reputation preceded him. A football star, and engaged to the Superintendent's daughter, who currently reigned as Miss Connecticut, Bob had been chosen to stay the summer at the Academy to welcome the new class of pledges. Every sailor who knew Bob said, "He'll be an admiral someday."

Forty years later, I watched President Obama present the State of the Union address, and noticed the shiny bald pate of my old bunkmate, Commandant of the Coast Guard, shaking the President's hand.

I updated the classified publications library, burned out of date secret codes in a barrel on deck, and learned to trust no one but Captain Black with national security. Untested, I awaited my opportunity to prove myself to the skipper and crew once the ship sailed. Knowing Papp would meet the Cutter once we arrived in Adak, this first trip would be my opportunity to shine. I passed on invitations to party ashore, and spent my free time studying in the wardroom, or just lying in my rack, reading.

Finally, in August, Captain Black set sailing orders for the voyage to Adak, two thousand nautical miles northwest. I had recently driven a comparable distance, from Michigan to the West Coast, in three days. The voyage to Alaska would take at least two weeks, traveling by sea, depending upon the wind, and the unpredictable weather of the North Pacific.

⊗

With Elsa twelve days old, my wife and child boarded a plane to San Francisco. The first plane ride for either young soul. Home for the next three weeks was a roll out sofa in Heather's closet sized, third floor apartment on California Street.

"So much better," she said over the poor connection, "I feel welcomed here. "But how am I going to get to Alaska?"

"You'll be fine," I replied, trying to convince myself.

⊗

"Take in one, three, and four," Jim relayed, while setting the stick ahead slow, "Hold two, left standard rudder."

Ironwood's black, steel stern walked slowly away from the pier. "All stop, rudder amidships, take in two," and he backed the stick down.

At the sound of one long blast on the ship's whistle, the crew of the Cutter *Ironwood* completed the evolution like a well-trained dance troupe. Each man knew his steps. The ship departed the safety of the dock, and entered the calm waters of Puget Sound. *Ironwood* became an island world unto herself. My heart filled with a sense of wonder as two thousand tons of steel floated naturally, effortlessly, into deep water.

With neither telephones nor other distractions of land, the crew settled in to the underway routine. Experienced hands guided, and chided, newcomers. A spanking young seaman apprentice, fresh from boot camp, searched the ship for the "relative bearing grease."

The Captain ordered a course north. Our route would take us in protected waters past Vancouver, British Columbia. About halfway through Canada, the cutter would be exposed to the Pacific from the west, until we entered the Inside Passage, near the Alaskan border, where barrier islands would protect the ship from the awesome power of the North Pacific Ocean.

cx

While I secured the gear in my stateroom aboard ship, Glenda packed her bags for another plane ride which would take them from Heather's warm apartment in San Francisco to Adak Island on the far end of the Aleutian Island archipelago.

Elsa, at the tender age of four weeks, would have an advantage lying peacefully in her mother's arms. She couldn't know the fear and apprehension her mother would feel. Two innocents were about to set out on a great journey, with my promise to meet them at the end their only reassurance.

cx

I was ordered to break-in on the bridge during the mid-watch, a four hour shift every twelve hours, running from midnight to 4:00 am, and again from noon until 4:00 pm. I kept a keen eye on the ship's Operations Officer, an Academy graduate who had been onboard a year. Terry would serve as my mentor, and teach me the art and skill required of a qualified Underway Officer of the Deck.

The first evening underway, I awaited the mid-watch up on the bridge with my camera. The cutter moved slowly northward, making twelve knots, while porpoise, whales, and sea birds glided around the hull. Water reflected life like a mirror, with the only movement formed by the ship's wake slowly radiating away. Sunset fell peacefully yet glorious across the deep blue surface. Quiet moments are all one can ask of the world at sea.

cx

Glenda and Elsa painstakingly made their own way north to Alaska. If I could only have known, if cell phones had existed, I still would have worried helplessly from the womb of my stateroom. They had flown to Seattle, where later, Glenda confided that she missed their stop on the underground tram several times, and frustrated and very alone, circled the airport continuously like electrons in a "do-loop." She had broken down and cried, until a friendly policeman helped her find the gate for the daily jet flight to Anchorage.

⌀

Darkness had fallen when Terry relieved Bos'n John Stubbs as Officer of the Deck, the Captain's direct conduit, responsible only to the Captain for running the ship, completing the mission, and the safety of all lives onboard. My job was to watch and learn.

Without a moon to light the way, the inland waterway between the barrier islands and the mainland glowed in a light show understood only by experienced hands. Distinguishing between lights marking the end of a dock, maybe a lighted buoy or lighthouse, or another ship bearing down, became confusing, and the disorientation became exhilarating in the solution. The safety of the Cutter and crew had been entrusted to Terry, to the solitary judgment of the Officer of the Deck.

Alternating my attention, I scanned the dark path ahead through binoculars, and then buried my eyes in the radar screen, searching for "contacts," other ships in the area that might cross our intended track line. I helped with navigational "fixes," or positions taken every fifteen minutes in confined, inland waters. Late in the four-hour watch, I walked out on the bridge wing, and studied the darkness as the cutter passed over an imaginary line in the water that marked the Canadian border.

I thought I saw a string of dull, low lying lights, just above the surface several miles ahead. Terry came out, looked through his binoculars, and chatted a bit. I assumed that Terry had also seen the lights, as he returned inside the bridge to check the latest ship's position. His face glowed, leaning over the chart table, illuminated only by soft red lights which are used exclusively on the bridge after dark, to protect one's night vision by not requiring pupils to adjust between light and dark. I remained outside, "above decks" and watched as the low-lying white lights drew closer. I tried to identify what the lights could be marking. The closer the lights came, the more concerned I grew. Finally, I called in to the bridge, "Terry, you do see those lights, right?"

Terry rushed to the bridge wing, raised his binoculars and shouted to the helmsman, "Holy Shit, Right Full Rudder."

A raft of logs had broken loose from a tow, and marked with dull lights around the perimeter, passed with the current closely down the port side of the cutter. Terry directed the helmsman, "Shift your rudder," then, "rudder amidships, steady on course three-five-eight degrees."

Ironwood rocked back and forth like water in a moving bathtub. A pan crashed to the deck in the galley below. Alarmed, Captain Black burst onto the bridge. Before the Old Man could ask, in a weak attempt at reassurance, Terry explained what had happened. The Captain, hearing only excuses, looked around the bridge, stopped, and made direct eye contact with me. No words needed to be spoken. I got the message, one I would never forget. When underway onboard a Coast Guard Cutter, never make assumptions. Be ever vigilant. And a life lesson, a small correction taken early will obviate the need for an emergency correction later on.

Old Man Black filled his pipe warily, fumbled impatiently with his lighter, and spent the rest of the mid-watch observing from his chair on the bridge.

❦

I could only imagine a young mother holding Elsa in a tiny, portable crib. Flying over the dark virgin forests of British Columbia, might she become lost in the darkness, and the wild vastness of space? Like me, had they bid a permanent farewell to the civilized world? Had they travelled to some unexplored end of the earth?

I knew my intrepid pair had challenges left to endure. The only way to cover the thousand mile route to Adak from Anchorage was by flying Reeves Aleutian Airways. Reeves, manned by reformed bush pilots, flew small, one and two engine props through some of the worst weather on earth. The airline's record was surprisingly good as a result of the pilots' skill in setting planes down in emergencies, on short, unrefined, rock and grass airfields that dotted the Aleutian Islands.

❦

Ironwood made her way north. We rolled a bit when we were exposed to westerly seas north of Vancouver, but the waves laid down once we entered the lee of Gwaii Haanas Island. I fell into the maze of shipboard routine: standing the mid-watch; sleeping until ten hundred hours, catching up on paperwork; eating a quick lunch; standing another four hours on bridge watch; grabbing dinner, and maybe a movie on the old reel-to-reel projector in the wardroom; then heading back to the bridge to begin the cycle again. I read when I found time, to take my mind off my wife and child, and lay in my bunk like a baby, rocking in a crib.

After crossing the US border north of Prince Rupert, BC, the Cutter entered the Inside Passage. Gorgeous green islands spread through the salt water, cut the winds, and provided a diversion. I studied wildlife on the varied shorelines through binoculars. We tied up in Ketchikan, as the Old Man wanted to catch a night's rest in port. A buddy from OCS had received orders to "Ketch" so we met up for dinner. Phone service was not available, and I really had no idea where to call anyway.

The Cutter arrived in Juneau at six in the morning the fifth day out of Seattle. I stayed up through the night not wanting to miss the mooring evolution. Once we tied up, Captain Black granted liberty to the crew for the twenty-four hour stay. I had made a friend in the Engineering Officer, Chief Warrant Officer Bob Klein. Bob was a crusty veteran of eighteen years at sea. He ran the ship's engineering plant, and supervised half the crew with a jaunty jaw and a quick mind. Technically, I outranked Bob, but would have been a fool to breathe it aloud.

Once the ship was safely moored, Bob exhaled smoke in a ring like my High School buddies just before a smart-assed comment. He grabbed me by the arm, "C'mon sailor, we're going ashore."

We walked through town to the Red Dog Saloon, a gritty sailor's bar, notorious throughout the Pacific fleet, and a place I'd heard the crew remember through infamous tales of late night exploits. A barmaid wearing jeans and a checkered flannel shirt, who must have weighed two-fifty, asked with a jolly smile, "What'll you have?"

Klein, his sly smile hidden behind a puff of smoke, ordered breakfast, and I followed his lead, a half-pound burger and a quart can of Foster's Ale. A sailor could count on the Red Dog anytime, day or night. After several more rounds, we waltzed back through town to the moorings, guided by the constant rumbling of the *Ironwood's* generators. I fell fast asleep before noon, and spent the remainder of the day asleep in my bunk.

⊰

    The four-hour plane ride from Anchorage to Adak lasted a day and a half for mother and baby daughter, and included an overnight, unscheduled layover in Cold Bay to replace linkage to the flaps. The oft-repaired plane finally landed on the volcanic, island outcropping of Adak, ten days in advance of the scheduled arrival of the Cutter *Ironwood*. After four days and three nights of travel, from San Francisco to Seattle, thence to points north and west, a young child-mother, holding her baby girl, stepped down onto the black, moon-like surface.

⊰

Ironwood and crew departed Juneau enroute Adak, an Island lying ten days and fifteen hundred miles west. Captain Black ordered the ship secured for sea, the North Pacific Ocean. We would be leaving the relative safety of the Inside Passage by midnight. I was reassigned to break in on the four to eight watch, traditionally known as the Navigator's watch. The sun often rises, and sets, on the four to eight. Historically, a ship's Navigator has taken positions with star fixes at both morning and evening twilight.

    I was assigned a new mentor, the ship's Bos'n, John Stubbs, a boisterous twenty-five year vet who didn't seem to like me much. Patient and soft spoken to a fault, I preferred to listen and learn rather than speak and sound foolish. Stubbs thought every Coast Guard officer should sound like General Patton, that force and volume commanded respect.

    "How did a pecker checker like you get assigned to a cutter in Alaska?"

    I burned inside, and felt the eyes of the bridge crew waiting for me to respond. I had never checked a pecker and never intended to. I had flown rescue missions on a helicopter crew, been valued for my medical knowledge, and responded to real emergencies. Who was this asshole? Hell, it took him twenty years to make Warrant Officer.

I demurred. I figured Stubbs was intimidated by my intelligence, and knew he was flabbergasted at my quick rise to rank. He responded with belittling comments while sucking on an old cigar through his ragged beard, a not too subtle reminder to Captain Black and the crew that he was the saltiest sailor onboard.

The Captain's standing orders, which are read as gospel by each incoming watch crew, advised vigilance for icebergs. The ship's track took us near Glacier Bay National Seashore. Ice, floating low in the water, will not always show up on radar. The morning watch passed without a sighting, and a pink dawn broke slowly over the eastern horizon.

The growing morning light revealed chunks of ice floating near the ship. The full sunrise unveiled a white cliff on the shoreline a mile north, rising several hundred feet above sea level, and topped by a glacier. A river of ice cascaded in slow motion, like a waterfall suspended in time. Days or weeks might pass before the weight of the ice became too heavy, and huge crystals plunged into the ocean below. Under Stubbs' discerning and disapproving eye, I piloted the cutter through ice floes, and kept the stern clear.

"Right five degrees rudder," as a white chunk of ice fell off to starboard.

"Shift your rudder," and another chunk was left to port.

I was back home in Michigan, on downhill skis, cutting my edges into the turns, gliding on a smooth slalom through moguls.

◁

The second day out of Juneau, Stubbs pushed too hard. At lunch around the wardroom table, he spouted off, targeting me, the boot Ensign, "Hey Pussy, when are you going to learn to give commands and act like an officer? You're in charge of the commissary right? This clam chowder is all potatoes."

I lowered my eyes to my plate to avoid meeting Stubbs'. I wondered if I could take him, knowing that my temper lay hidden well beneath my calm exterior.

Captain Black raised his eyes from his soup, and silently stared Stubbs down. The same stare I had received on the bridge the first night out.

Nothing needed to be said. I raised my head. From that moment on, a cool but professional relationship existed between Stubbs and me, though, in retrospect, he had taught me to stand my ground.

❧

Glenda's travails eased when the Captain's wife met the plane. She had also arranged for our house to be ready. Some of the other wives cooked a welcome dinner. The Island of Adak would be her home for the foreseeable future. The military style, flat roofed, duplex ranch was built on gimbals so that the house would roll with earthquakes that frequently rocked the island. Reinforced glass windows could not be opened, a precaution against wind gusts that commonly reached one hundred miles per hour.

❧

The edges of days and nights at sea merged, and became as undefined as the point where water ends and the sky begins. Hours of monotony were broken only by moments of beauty revealed. I learned to apply my book knowledge of the art of navigation to the real world. My fixes were accurate, my reports to the Captain crisp. Stubbs grudgingly acknowledged my competence. Seven days out of Juneau, he told the Captain that I was ready to stand before the Board for certification as an Officer of the Deck in open waters. I passed the Review Board with a perfect score.

A new sense of freedom, accomplishment, and responsibility came with standing my own watch. The Captain assigned me the Navigator's watch. I was in my element, watching the sun set quietly into the western horizon each evening, only to watch it rise again in the east the following morning, while most of the fifty man crew slept trusting, in their bunks below decks.

❧

Glenda settled in, cleaned the already clean house, and began unpacking a few boxes of personal things. The duplex was mostly furnished. The government avoided the expense of shipping furniture from the lower forty-eight. Carefully, she placed her watercolors on the walls while Elsa slept. Whenever Glenda sat down for a meal, Elsa would wake and cry, and only her mother's breast could calm her. In a few days, Glenda made their den safe from the wild, outside world.

∾

I wanted to be named Navigator, and had a chance to help my cause when the cutter's electronic navigation systems, both LORAN and radar, failed just three days before reaching Adak. The ship's generator had spiked, and burned circuits in the sensitive equipment.

The ship's course lay far south of the Aleutian Island chain, and we were unable to see recognizable landmarks for a visual position. Fresh from celestial navigation practice back at Yorktown, I found two sextants buried in a cabinet in the radio room. "Come with me," I ordered the Quartermaster of the Watch, as the sun fell below the western horizon and twilight set in.

I checked the star diagrams in Bowditch's Practical Navigator, "See that star" pointing out Betelgeuse, Orion's head. Put the star in your sight and adjust the sextant angle until the star appears to be on the line of the horizon. I'll do the same with Antares, and Jupiter. Say, "Mark" when you're ready, then hold the angle steady until I can record the other readings."

I took two more sightings, and recorded four, separated by sixty degrees, to provide a good cross. "We'll take sextant angles each morning and evening twilight until the electronics are fixed," and I retreated to the chartroom to reduce the angles. The Old Man looked on from the bridge and smiled. When the cutter approached land two days later, a visual position proved my celestial fixes accurate, to within a hundred yards, a miniscule dot in the vast North Pacific Ocean.

∾

The shipboard routine buffered my constant concern for my new family. Duty forced me to put those thoughts aside, knowing I was helpless to respond. I could only trust that my wife and child were safe and healthy, and settled on Adak by now.

I did not worry alone. As the ship drew closer to Adak, anticipation grew amongst the crew. The confined air below decks was thick with uneasy apprehension. The crew had travelled so far, in miles and in experience, every last sailor, even the Captain, and we were so close to home. No one uttered a word.

The Cutter Ironwood cleared Amchitka Island in the early morning of the day we were scheduled to arrive at homeport. Venturing into the open Bering Sea, the ship lost the lee of the island and was hit by strong winds from the northwest. The seas picked up intensity, rolled the cutter relentlessly, and sent fresh cold spray over the bow. The Captain ordered the crew to stay below decks and increased propeller turns. An uncomfortable, seemingly never-ending period ensued, while the ship banged into twelve foot waves. Shudders echoed through the thick steel hull. I wedged myself tightly between the forward bridge bulkhead and the annunciator panel, clenched my thigh muscles, and looked out at the churning sea.

In late afternoon, the ship entered the lee of Adak Island, and the wind and seas began to diminish. Mt. Moffett, a recently active volcano rising thirty-nine hundred feet above sea level, appeared stately in the west. The black volcanic rock, adorned with white snow at the peak, sheltered the cutter from the northwest gales.

Ironwood made the wide turn into Sweeper's Cove, the only navigable, protected harbor along Adak Island's two hundred mile coastline. Bald eagles flew escort, gliding from nests on the gray cliffs which rose on the southern side of the Bay, and landed effortlessly on hills overlooking the moorings.

Families stood arm in arm, watching on the dock, and the crew manned the rails, as the Captain moored the cutter alongside the pier. From the bridge wing, I searched faces that grew ever closer. The cutter glided effortlessly, slowly, toward solid ground, just as she had left the cradle of the dock in Seattle weeks earlier. Lost time disappeared in a moment.

Finally, unmistakably, I saw her waist-long, dark, braided hair. I saw my wife, holding Elsa covered in a soft blanket, protecting the baby from the ocean breeze. I saw my family, and watched worry, wonder, and guilt dissolve. I had reached a new home, the Island of Adak, the Birthplace of the Winds.

I had become a sailor, and learned a sailor's hard lesson. I longed for the comfort of dry land, yet yearned for the time I would again depart, and cast off the binding double braid.

A sailor has two homes, the sea, and the shore, where sometimes, loved ones wait.

PRIEST ROCK

I looked out across the angry waters of Lliuliuk Bay from the bridge of the Cutter *Ironwood*. Through an impending dark sky, my eyes focused on a haunting, black monolith, shaped like a monstrous, druid priest. A cape of dread covered me when a glint of light flashed from atop the rock.

"That's Priest Rock." The Captain had noticed me staring. "The light is weak, the batteries are failing."

We continued our slow approach into Dutch Harbor after ten days at sea. The crew, cold and tired, needed a night ashore. "Dutch", a second home for *Ironwood*, provided a safe port set in the geographic center of the Aleutians. The location reduced the distance for trips east to Kodiak, or north on the Bering toward Nome. Excitement increased with the crew's anticipation of spending a night tied up in port following a rough few days on the Bering Sea.

The navigational light mounted on Priest Rock marked the entrance for shipping on the way into Dutch Harbor. Rather than a traditional light-house, a steel framed structure, fifty feet high, supported a Fresnel lens at the top. The lens was powered by a pack of batteries stored watertight in the concrete base of the light tower. The light warned the crab fleet to stay off the rocks, that came awash at low tide. Sailor's wisdom, spun below decks, says the priest sometimes moves his eyes as ships pass. Avoid his gaze, for if the priest looks at you, trouble will likely follow.

Captain Black watched closely as I maneuvered *Ironwood* to the timber dock in Dutch Harbor just before dark. Most of the crew wandered across the brow, and spent the night drinking beer at the Elbow Room, an old Quonset hut-turned-bar that smelled like the patrons; crabbers, and the sailors between ships, who cleaned the crabs for market.

I watched as King Crabs by the hundreds, captured alive, cascaded from the nets of the crab boats onto the deck of a factory ship. The old iron transport had her engines removed, and moored permanently to the dock, served as a floating kitchen. The crabs sometimes measured six feet in diameter from claw to claw.

Rubber-booted men tossed these royal crustaceans into a parboiling vat, and dipped them out of the stew with wire baskets. The succulent white meat, was hand-picked from the shell, and molded into three foot long blocks, two inches wide and four inches thick, an edible two-by-four. The blocks of pure meat were shipped frozen to the lower forty-eight on refrigerated transports.

Olympia, the only beer available at the Elbow Room, came in weekly on refrigerator ships making the return trip from Seattle or Anchorage after delivering the crab meat. The few women who hung around the bar were as rough as the corrugated steel walls. Watch out for the knife if you looked crosswise at them, or welched on the agreed fee. The bargain was sure to include the Clap. I kept my distance.

&

The Old Man called me up to the Cabin the next morning. The crew needed rest after the tough steam to Dutch from Adak. But Priest Rock needed a recharge, a new set of batteries. "Tom," he said, "take the young Bos'n and the dory launch and see if you can get it done. We'll give the other boys a day off."

George was a handsome young boatswain's mate of Greek descent. His black hair and beard curled in a style just past regulation length. He and I climbed in, and the duty crew lowered the cutter's motor surf boat into the dark water of the harbor. In 1976, with solar power still under development, four, forty-pound batteries, similar to those used in a car but bolted together in a wooden rack, were required to power a navigational light for a year. We eased the small boat up against the Cutter's black hull just below the buoy deck. The Chief motioned to the boom operator to raise the battery pack up off the deck. I held the small boat steady while George guided the weight down, balanced the pack, and tied it off. As he tossed us the bow line, the Chief called out, "Remember, this is the last set of batteries between here and Kodiak."

George Argyros looked like a young Greek god standing at the helm of the dory. Unalaska Channel was framed by long dead volcanoes, which had eroded into peaked islands of gray and black stone. Priest Rock lay a few miles off shore to the east. The bay rolled in long, greasy, swaying swells. I took the tiller while George prepared the battery pack. The swells, as if alive, wanted to take the dory's head away in no particular direction. I could not allow the dory to become crosswise to the four foot sea or we might lose the batteries over the side.

Running a small boat in this sea was dangerous, exacting, and unforgiving work. Priest Rock Light, positioned to keep ships off the rocks, would perhaps save the life of one of the young crabbers we had shared beers with the night before. No one, not even a good swimmer, could survive long in the cold of the Bering Sea.

The waves rose, then fell as the dory drew closer to shore. There was no dock to moor the dory at Priest Rock. With George running the boat, I timed the waves and stepped ashore on the smooth, slippery black rock surface just before the dory was sucked back out with the swell. Once I stabilized my footing, George cast me a line. I caught the bitter end before it disappeared back into the sea, and tied the dory off to steel angle iron at the base of the tower. The Priest hovered fifty feet above. All my strength was required to secure the end of the line. The Priest watched my every move. I avoided his eyes.

I held the line, and inched my way back down the incline to the water's edge. George eased the dory toward shore, timing the swell. He kept power on the throttle to hold the boat against the rocks, while I reached to unload the battery pack. If I lost the batteries to the sea, a plane would have to deliver a new set from Kodiak. The Old Man would have my ass, and the Admiral would have his.

The dory held well, and the swell provided a brief window of opportunity. I stood on a reasonably level outcropping, maybe two feet wide. With one hand on the line, and the other on the dory's wheel, George tried to tie a safety line around the battery pack. As he edged forward to the bow he lost the wheel. The dory was pulled away from shore with the swell.

The ocean dropped suddenly, as if someone had opened a drain. The dory rolled with the swell, and was sucked down and away. I grabbed the two-hundred-pound battery pack from the bow of the dory. I hugged it like a woman and held on, fighting the power of the sea. My leather boots should have slipped on the wet rock. I held not just the batteries, but the weight of the boat against the swell.

I held back the sea. For a moment that lasted an eternity, I felt a supernatural strength run through my arms, and willed the dory back to shore.

George regained the helm of the dory. I lifted the battery pack on to the rock with a guttural sigh, thinking, "Neither the Chief, nor the Old Man, nor anyone else will ever know."

But George and I will know, and will always remember. George climbed ashore, and we finished the job under the watchful eyes of the Priest.

I do not know why the cold dark sea failed to gather me in that day. I held on to life as I held the battery pack. I waited for the sea to subside, for the swell to return, and lay the dory safely against the rocky shore. Until a test arrives, a man cannot know his own strength.

I cast the dory off, turned, and stared the priest down.

I thought I saw him smile.

ALASKAN REFLECTION

I was at sea, the Bering Sea, north of the Aleutians, in the spring of 1976. Coastal Alaska harbored a land of pipefitters, wildcatters, sailors from the king crab fleet, and any young swinging dick who had the balls to travel north. My Alaska is ingrained as a time for adventurers who built the pipeline, relived the Wild West, and thanked fate for the opportunity.

Pipefitters spent months toiling on the North Slope, and sailors floated on the Bering Sea, each to earn a few days off in Fairbanks, Anchorage, or maybe even Juneau. Every man carried a sidearm, for the bears, yet guns were seldom drawn in a bar fight. Bare fists decided the argument while doing no lasting harm. In six months, a young man not afraid to work could pack away some dough; maybe live on what he saved for a couple years back home in the lower forty-eight, and mine memories to last a lifetime.

I sailed as Navigator on a sea going buoy tender, the Cutter *Ironwood*. Notwithstanding having survived the previous fall on the Bering Sea, old time Alaskans still called me a tenderfoot. All through November, the one hundred-eighty foot steel ship had endured fifty foot waves fueled by steady winds of forty to sixty knots, and gusts reaching one hundred. For days at a time, the crew lived a torturous routine, lying wedged in bunks, just holding on, and trying to sleep before the next watch.

"One hand for the ship, one for yourself," the rule, while the ship rolled thirty to forty degrees, first one way, and then the other. Pans crashed in the galley below decks, and the cook cut the menu back to peanut butter and saltine crackers. Though tended on a line, even the surefooted young boatswain's mate of the watch slipped and slid on his rounds, and surfed on green water that covered the outside decks.

UNALASKA

For three long days and nights, the Cutter had plowed into a heavy sea just to maintain headway. Our mission was to service a lighthouse on Unalaska Island, and we needed the swells to ease below four feet to drop the small boat over the side, and safely send a crew ashore.

I had the deck and conn of the ship on the morning watch. Just after dawn, the wind began to die. The swells still rolled from the west between twenty-five and thirty feet. The blue-green sea takes time to recover from a three day blow. I spun the handle on the sound powered phone with the lever notched to the Old Man's Cabin, "Captain, the wind's letting up a bit. We might be able to make the turn south toward Unalaska."

The old man struggled up the ladder from his cabin to the cutter's bridge. Unshaven and ragged, his tired eyes betrayed seasickness. Anyone who says they have sailed the Bering Sea in autumn's fierce glory and never fallen to the sickness, tells a liar's tale. Finding his sea legs, he walked over to the chart table, and with thumb and forefinger, checked the position I had plotted. He looked up at the anemometer, which pulsed between twelve and eighteen knots. The ship rocked. The Captain turned toward the glass portals lining the front of the bridge, and steadied his gait with a hand on the bulkhead before climbing up into his chair.

"Make the pipe."

The microphone hung on the aft bulkhead. I walked over, raised the mike to my mouth, practiced the exact words, took a deep breath, and confidently announced throughout the ship,

"Secure all hatches, stow any loose gear. Stand by for heavy rolls as the ship comes about."

I figured the Old Man would take the Conn for the crucial maneuver of turning the ship in heavy seas. One mistake and she'd go broadside in the swell, maybe capsize.

"Pick your wave," the Old Man said, his eyes penetrating my soul.

My concentration absolute, I studied the swells, timed the period between peaks, and tried to discern a pattern. The waves were steady and strong, and looking out the forward ports from the bottom of a swell, I saw a crest break above the deck of the flying bridge. That meant the seas rolled higher than thirty-seven feet.

I was a kid, floating in the salt water of the Atlantic, watching waves on a warm summer afternoon, waiting for the big one, the one I could ride all the way to shore with my chest and arms extended, while I flew with the pull of the moon. Dumped near the shallows, tumbled and turned, sand and tar in my hair, and looking up at the translucent surface, I held my breath.

"Here we go," I announced, glancing at the Old Man.

"Don't stop once you start."

I recalled the same advice I had received from my Uncle Doug in a muddy cornfield. And I remembered the outcome when I failed to heed the warning.

I let the ship rise to the top of the swell. As we began to surf down the back side toward an endless, greenish-blue valley, I rammed the throttle control for both main engines hard ahead, and called out to the helmsman, "Left full rudder."

We plunged into the deep valley, and doused the forecastle in green sea. The propeller broke free of the water surface, and cavitated, sending shudders through the iron hull like shock waves. But the bow rose again, an upward force like a Blue Whale rising, into the coming swell. Two of the steel stanchions ringing the foc'sle' broke loose, and hung only by the safety chain.

The Cutter climbed up a mountainous slope, climbed and turned, climbed, and began to turn. I urged her on from the bellows of my stomach. Almost to the peak, almost turned, but sideways, heading for the trough.

The Old Man jumped down from his chair, his eyes wide with fear. I rammed the throttle forward again. We needed one more turn of the prop. The brass arm on the hull angle indicator pushed past fifty degrees, the ship closer to going over than staying upright.

All fifty souls aboard hung on to the ship as she rocked. Our lives hid in the balance between sky and water. Suspended in air, I looked down at the sea. With a sudden jerk, flotation overcame gravity, and like a slingshot, balance returned. The good Cutter *Ironwood* rolled sharply back to the right, rocked again to the left, and settled into a rush down the swell.

"Ease your rudder. Now rudder amidships. Steady on course zero-nine-five. Make sure you adjust for the following swell."

The deep breath I had held, escaped, and I was a kid again, catching the biggest wave of the day, my arms and chest flying free through the air.

In a few short hours, the sun returned, and the sea flattened. The only waves in sight stirred in the wake of the Cutter as she sliced through fluid magic, riding high and dry on the charcoal-blue Bering Sea.

SEA LION ROCK

"No way we can land the bird here. You'll have to ride the sling down."

The chopper flew high above an island, a granite outcropping several miles north of the Aleutian chain. I looked down at the icy waters of Unimak Pass crashing into the base of stone walls, which rose from the water straight up three hundred feet on three sides of the monolith. On the top, a plateau, perhaps twenty yards in diameter, had been formed by some demonic geologic force. Also on top stood a navigational light, a lens mounted on scaffolding which added another twenty feet, and allowed the light to be visible to mariners far north on the Bering Sea.

The light marked the eastern limits of Unimak Pass. A light meant to keep the king crab fleet safely off the rocks and shoals that surrounded the treacherous pass, where waters of the Bering merge with the North Pacific Ocean. A light gone dark.

The fourth side, the southern exposure of Sea Lion Rock, flowed gently down to the sea, like a natural ramp, or a slide where children glide laughing into a pool. But here, the creatures gliding and laughing, sunning on the slope, were sea lions. Hundreds. Too thick to count, perhaps eight hundred.

"Take the Very pistol, those suckers can be mean," the pilot warned, pointing to the flare gun and speaking through the headset, the only way to communicate above the drone on board the twin engine jet helicopter.

I fit the hoisting sling around my head and shoulders, loaded a flare shell into the pistol, checked my pack for the tools I would need to repair the light, and for additional shell cartridges, and shackled the sling into the eye on the wire hoist. The flares are meant to scare off these half-sea, half-land monsters. Hope they work.

The pilot moved the chopper sideways until I could see the plateau directly below the door. He steadied the noisy plane in a hover. I climbed out the door, suspended fifty feet above the rock, and while the crewman slowly let out wire, I watched a mass exodus of flesh slide, and splash into the sea.

Upon reaching the surface, I pulled off the sling, and the crewman retracted my escape wire. A few sea lions loitered at the bottom of the slope two hundred feet away. We exchanged wary looks.

Using the access ladder, I climbed up the structure, and set my tools out on the corrugated steel platform. A gauge indicated no problem with the power supply, plenty of voltage, so I unhooked the daylight control eye, and the light began blinking in a four second pattern. Ah, bad daylight control eye. Got one!

Reaching into the pack, I noticed a few more sea lions flapping their way back up the stone ramp. Then more, and more, in a mad rush to slippery land. They climbed over each other, pushing and shoving like shoppers on Black Friday.

And I saw why. In the blue water just off shore lurked two ominous, black dorsal fins. Orca. Killer whales.

With renewed vigor, I screwed on the new eye, checked and tightened the connections, and climbed down from the iron structure. The ramp, a mass of life, oozed toward me like a lava flow. I waved my arms to get the pilot's attention, not able to fire a warning shot, not wanting to send a lion to death in a whale's jaw.

A few bold shapes ambled closer, ignoring the whine of the chopper directly overhead. I looked up at the yellow sling that descended slowly, in dream time, and knew that the wire must first touch the ground, or built-up static would send a shock through my arm. But I also had to grab the clip before the helicopter lurched in the wind, and my escape swung away.

The wire clip bounced off the ground like a rock skipping on a pond. I lunged, and in a single motion, caught the cold steel clip and snapped it through the eye on my vest. And suddenly, I flew, up and away through the air, suspended, hanging by a wire above black and white shapes, while crooners of the land and sea moaned, just beneath the soles of my boots.

MIDNIGHT SUN

"**D**amn, you know you can't even get a beer in this town," I over-heard our chopper pilot, Commander Rick Denton over the headset, as he landed in a rocky field that served as the airport in the north Alaskan coastal town of Kotzebue. "Native land."

Lieutenant Bill Short, the young cocky co-pilot, in a southern drawl, not to be denied, "Not to worry, I have some fine Kentucky bourbon in my duffel."

We'd flown in from Nome, a sunny day trip across the Seward Peninsula. I was still an Ensign, a year out of OCS, but a Mustang, having come up out of the enlisted ranks, and served on the Coast Guard Cutter *Ironwood*. The ship had thrown a shaft bearing, then limping back to port, burnt up a main generator coil. The only shipyard capable of a fix was a two-week steam back in Seattle. The lighthouses marking the port entries on Alaska's North Slope needed to be serviced in the short window of summer, during the time of the midnight sun.

Captain Black had assigned me this duty three weeks earlier, on the bridge of the cutter during the mid-watch, midnight til' four am, as I dodged floating chunks of ice in the Bering Strait. We watched the sun dip below the horizon momentarily, due north, and rise within the same hour, ten degrees east.

"Counting on you Tom, " the Old Man had confided, "take George and the supplies you'll need. I'll have a helicopter from Kodiak pick you up in Nome."

While *Ironwood* limped toward Seattle, Georgey and I had spent those three weeks on the vacation of a lifetime, and seen back country Alaska through unique eyes. A Boatswains Mate Second Class, good-looking with black hair and a curly beard, and about my age, George had been my traveling companion before on other adventures, and had become a trusted friend. We had crossed the forbidden line of familiarization between an officer and his enlisted charge. This trip, we had serviced twelve lights, from the Norton Sound to Barrow, gone through two shifts of helicopter crews, and as the Bicentennial approached on July 4th, 1976, we had just two more lights to service.

"Underway at dawn," Denton ordered, "I want to have you back to Nome tomorrow, so we can get home to Kodiak by the fourth."

For all the worry, the trip flying over the De Long Mountain range had the feel of a sightseeing adventure. The sun came out early, and the temperature quickly rose to the sixties. Only wilderness lay in our path north from Kotzebue to the light at Cape Lisburne on the Arctic Ocean. Standard operating procedures for the chopper called for following the coastline at all times, keeping the shore in sight. A forced landing inland, away from help, meant trouble, isolation, and a survival situation.

"Hell, it's a nice day, let's cut across." The tough-looking, bearded Denton had flown in Alaska for seven years. Short's eyes opened wide. I sat in the jump seat between them ready for anything, and looked back in the cabin to see Georgey smiling.

We cleared an unnamed rocky peak, and settled into a cruise over the long open valley of the Noatak River, which flowed west and south toward the Chukchi Sea, a bay off the Arctic Ocean. Denton kept the chopper low, and we swayed through the air, and enjoyed the vast open space. Soft tundra, and lichen in greens and purples and reds, spread for miles, broken occasionally by stands of aspen. The swollen river flowed in bends and curves patterned like letters in an old English script.

Denton brought the plane up a couple hundred feet to clear a small ridge, and before us, another river flowed brown, not patterned, but wide and straight, and extended for miles. We observed as thousands of caribou migrated south, plunged through creeks and rivers in this summer-spring of the north, and searched for food.

We followed above the brown river to the source, where only a few stragglers remained. "There's a nice shed," Denton announced after spotting a six foot wide rack, shed antlers, lying on the mossy ground. He pulled up on the stick just before we set the wheels down softly on the tundra floor. "George, jump out and grab those antlers."

Georgey climbed back in, and stowed the antlers in a spare battery box along with some of the other treasures of our scavenger hunt. *Just boys out for a day in the woods, collecting stuff, except our toys had changed.* Denton raised the stick, we lifted off, and as he increased power, the chopper's nose dipped before rising sharply.

"Hey" I called out over the headset, "something's moving near those trees." Denton headed toward the shapes in motion.

Short grabbed his camera while Denton put the helicopter in a circular hover. Before our eyes, a feline head appeared too big for its body, with pointed ears. A yellow lynx, larger than life, caught, and took down a young caribou. Attention on his prize, the lynx looked up at our noisy flying machine, and disdaining interest, smiled like the Cheshire Cat.

We made Cape Lisburne around noon, landed in an open field, and shut down. Georgey and I carried our gear out to the lighthouse on a natural rock breakwall that extended into the Arctic Ocean. Denton and Short stretched, and took a walk into the Inupiat village. We cleaned up the lens, replaced batteries, and checked all the connections, a routine service. The pilots were still off sightseeing, so we kicked back and enjoyed sandwiches and a can of Coke out of the cooler.

We lifted off in mid-afternoon, and followed the coast along the Arctic Ocean northeast toward Point Lay, a small Native village, where a lighthouse marked the mouth of the Kokolik River at the point the river enters the sea. Denton again kept the plane low and flew slowly. Our quarry consisted of glass balls, multi-colored floats used by Japanese fishing boats to float nets. And perhaps, we might come across a walrus, washed ashore, having died naturally but with tusks intact.

Denton landed several times along the way, just long enough to beach comb, and collect glass balls. I found one, a shade of light purple and the size of a volleyball, and several luminous, squash-sized balls. We collected nearly a hundred green glass floats, like baseballs washed up on shore. The pilots both looked enviously at my violet find, as I carefully wrapped the purple ball in canvas, and set it in the box for safe keeping. The Old Man would appreciate the treasure.

Twenty miles east of Point Lay, the Kukpowruk River meanders parallel to the Arctic Ocean. The presence of man became evident along the sandy isthmus separating fresh water from the frothy salt sea. We looked out on walrus, killed, and strewn along the beaches, tusks sawn off. I counted twelve between Lisbourne and Point Lay. And cutting through the tundra leading away from the beach, snowmobile tracks led to Native villages. For hundreds of years, Inupiat have hunted walrus, whales and seals, but for the meat and oil, not only the ivory. The advent of tourist shops in Nome, Fairbanks, and Anchorage, and in seaports around the world where ivory trinkets are sold, increased the plunder, while twelve foot long carcasses rotted, wasted on the shores of the Arctic.

"The weather report just came in, not good. Let's get moving," Denton ordered from our last beach stop, and in minutes we landed at Point Lay in a field surrounded by small clapboard houses, built in a circle. Rusting snowmobiles littered the ground, and dogs of every make and hue wandered up, looking for a handout.

The humidity had become oppressive, and mosquitos swarmed around my head. We walked quickly toward the lighthouse which sat on a spit formed by the river current fusing into the Arctic Ocean. Momentarily, I gazed back toward shore, stood on the edge of the sea, and looked back upon the stark, natural landscape.

The light, reported out several days earlier, was AC power, fueled by a diesel generator in the village. Tuning up the light should have been an easy task. Georgey climbed up the structure with his tool bag, and reached the top. The clouds thickened, but no more than the cloud of bugs that followed Georgey's every move. He broke down the light, tested every part, and put it back together. No luck.

"What about changing the daylight control sensor?" I called up.

"Let's try it," George replied, "but I don't have a spare."

"There's two more back at the plane. I'll go."

I ran the half mile to the helicopter where Denton sat, anxious, worried. "We gotta' go, man, weather's coming."

I hustled back to the light with a mutt chasing at my ankles, and sweating, tossed the control up to Georgey. Still no light. He checked the circuit with the meter. The new control had burned out. George climbed down. We sat and reasoned, knowing our time was short, not wanting to spend the night in the chopper in some isolated village. I looked around the base of the light, and noticed a circuit cover hanging by one screw. "Put the meter on that circuit, where the power comes in."

George touched the probes. Sparks flew. The wires coming in had melted together, and reversed polarity to the circuit in the light. I hit the outside breaker. Georgey spliced in new cables, climbed up, and replaced the last daylight control. I energized the main breaker.

Voila! We gathered our gear and ran to the plane.

Denton was not happy. He wanted no part of my reasonable explanation for the delay. We took off with purpose into darkening skies. All heads strained forward, all eyes stared with concern, dead ahead.

"We have no choice," I heard Denton cough gruffly into the mike, "we'll have to go overland to make Nome tonight." The pilots had pushed the limit, exceeded legal hours at the throttle. Flying as fast as the chopper could take us but into a growing headwind, we rose to eight hundred feet, and bulleted over and across the De Long Mountains, not pausing to look at the caribou herds far below. We flew across the Kotzebue Sound, then carried due south, again over land, into the wilds of the Seward Peninsula. One hundred air miles remained to reach Nome, and safe ground.

Rain started to fall, and on the western horizon, lightning illuminated thick grey clouds. The land of the midnight sun became too dark, too early. Fog eliminated visibility. About halfway across the peninsula, the LORAN positioning module failed, "probably static and rain," Short observed.

I sat in the jump seat, and suddenly, through the low lying clouds, saw green peaks much too close. "Georgey," I began into the headset, wanting him to secure the gear in back in case we had to land, when Short rapped my chin with two fingers, hard enough to get my attention. The look in his eyes warned, keep the channel clear.

A navigator myself, and experienced in dealing with equipment malfunction, and having adapted to finding my way without instruments, I hadn't been too worried. The snap on my jaw awakened me to a new world. These pilots, experienced, senior officers, were not magicians, not superheroes. I knew as much as they did about where we were.

And one short comment confirmed my thoughts. Denton looked over at Short, then at me, "Well, there's a creek we can follow, it's bound to lead us down to the sea."

A communal sigh of relief could almost be heard when through the fog ahead, the alluvial sand shores of Norton Sound appeared, and in an hour, we landed at the airport in Nome, at midnight, July 3rd, 1976.

A few weeks later, I had made the trip back to homeport in Adak. Our battery boxes arrived by C-130 transport. The Old Man was anxious for some souvenirs, and, of course, I had talked up our bounty. I opened two battery boxes, and in with our tool bags, rolled a few dozen small, green, glass balls. My purple-hued orb was missing.

A pirate's treasure, wantonly pillaged by pilots.

PART TWO

CARIBBEAN DREAMS

GRAND CAYMAN

North shore, like a park, third world.
light fishing vest, bathing suit,
old canvas sneakers, mollusks.
Wade into the salt sea, calm,
protected by the barrier reef.
Tufts of wet, muddled sand kicked up from the bottom,
a small crab, looks like a small crab,
tied on clear leader.
Cast back toward the shore, under overhanging
mangroves, where bonefish fly, stealth jets,
detected by a ripple.

The ladies lie on the south shore, the wide, clean, seven mile beach.
One tans golden in the sun, refreshes,
washes in azure sea, coconut cream. Taste, sour, body.
Another walks, sunhat and lace dress, collects shells
and sea glass.

Rays play beneath my feet.
If the bonefish are jet fighters,
manta are B-1 bombers, spiny tails for bombs.
My fly reel spins. Chest deep in ocean, I lift my arms
take up slack with my left hand, loop the white floating line,
a lariat suspended, spin the reel with my right, tension on the fish,
always tension on the line.
A ray hovers below, step carefully in canvas shoes.
The final few yards of line drawn in by hand.
Remove the crab from the mouth of a yellow jack,
wiggle him about in the sea, he swims away.
Dinner?
No, thanks anyway,
the ladies have reservations, on the south shore.

NASSAU

"Fifteen-two, fifteen-four, ain't no more," says Ralph Cromley, the Engineering Officer, looking over my shoulder, while setting down another green bottle of Beck's on the small square table in front of me. Cromley reminds me of Popeye with those arms, muscles that bulge between his elbows and wrists, and his boisterous laugh. I want him on my side in a fight.

"Gotcha this time, Ex," replies Joe, the Bos'n, broad and also tough, in a different way. "Two-four-six-eight, and eight's a dozen." Joe, close to retirement after 30 years at sea, pegs around the top of the board. "Ex" is what they call me when we're drinking, short for "XO" aboard ship, the Cutter *Sweetgum*. I'm the Executive Officer, second in command.

The late Seventies, and we've been running the Bahama Banks for a few weeks now, half-looking for Haitian refugees. Fresh off an all-night search, I took the bridge while we tracked an old wooden sailboat into Freeport. Women and kids, starving and puking, hung over the sides of a boat, with no freeboard between souls and the deep.

This AIDS epidemic is just taking off, and the crew, without speaking, seems relieved that the refugees put ashore out of our jurisdiction. Big rollers from the east rocked the ship silly when we made the turn south toward Nassau Harbor. But all is well about the decks, with three days off ashore to savor my first liberty in the Caribbean.

The Old Man slides up to the bar. He always drinks alone, seven and seven, never more than two. With his black hair and dark complexion, he's got that hunched over, sailor at the bar look. I think he puts it on, like Bogart in Casablanca.

Joe smiles, takes a pull on his beer. It's my deal, my crib, so I shuffle and let go, turn over a six, three sevens and two eights. Joe has to fill my crib with a six and an eight, and the flip card, the last seven. Joe pegs four, leaving him just short of the skunk painted on the board. I count twenty-one and twenty-four, waltz around Joe from behind, and peg out, "Skunked. That'll be two beers each, Boats."

Joe gets up grumbling, and even buys the Captain his second whiskey. The Old Man sits down with us for a four-man game, me and Cromley team up. He doesn't seem to like me much, the Old Man. I came up from the ranks like him, but he made Chief as an enlisted man, and then went straight to Lieutenant. Now he's in line for full Commander, and a two hundred-ten foot Cutter his next tour. But he likes me more than Academy pukes, young Ensigns right out of school, know-it-all college kids. The Old Man never went to college.

We've got three Ensigns, all from the Academy, on the *Sweetgum*. My job is to train them, train them to take my job. The Old Man's job is to train me the same way. With *Sweetgum's* homeport in Mayport, Florida, we always get the top graduates. Two spanking new sailors this trip, Wiz, the Academy-class valedictorian, who's watching us play cribbage, and nursing his one beer so the Old Man will see he's not a drinker. Number four in his class, Jay, is back watching the ship, and the sparse shore duty crew. Jay is young and cocky, can't tell him anything.

The Ensigns are always bitching to me about the Old Man, "Old School, doesn't he know we've had four years of college?"

"He knows. Get back to your duties." I don't usually agree with the Captain, but keep it to myself, never show him up. He's right though, four years of college doesn't make a sailor. So you can see how this card game is strained a bit.

We've been in this old corner bar, drinking since eleven in the morning, and decide to walk back to the ship for dinner rather than spend money on a restaurant. I kind of had a taste for conch fritters, but head back anyway.

Laughing and tossing insults, we stroll past the tiki-huts, where three Tee-shirts can be had for about ten bucks American. Homemade cotton Rasta dolls, the kind you can poke pins into, just four bucks, and those straw things that lock fingers together sell for about a quarter. They only take Caribs, though, so I'll have to find a bank before I can buy souvenirs.

"The bank is on Nassau Street, over a few blocks," the Old Man points out. I'm thinking, he's almost human. "Over there with the high roller jewelry stores. They'll be happy to take your money." Maybe I'll walk back after dinner.

Bumping and laughing, we reach the pier complex as twilight sets in. A cruise ship has just docked, and sunburnt tourists hang over the rails, itching to get ashore. A good night for the casino over on Paradise Island.

Cromley, who's been here before, says, "Hey, if we put on our whites, the cruise ship Captain will let us into the top deck party. God damn, French and German stewardesses, hot to trot."

The main pier, built of trees, hewn to twelve by twelve inches, is a hundred feet wide and nearly a quarter of a mile long. Two wings extend to the west. I had docked the *Sweetgum* on the far wing. We can't see much in the fading light, but there was no electrical hook-up, so the ship's generator is rumbling and scratching, like a foghorn guiding us home.

I look to the west near the first pier wing, where we hear the generator sound, and see two red aircraft warning lights, just like *Sweetgum's*, "Must be another cutter in port."

Wiz, the young Ensign, plodding behind, says, "I don't think so."

I look to the far pier wing, and see no shape, no lights, "What the fuck, over."

The Old Man breaks out ahead with purpose, and I follow dutifully. The others hang back, knowing this won't be good. The *Sweetgum* is not where we left her.

Jay stands atop the gangway, proud and smiling, and arrogant as ever. "The Port Authority made us shift berths. I sounded the whistle for recall but no one came."

The Old Man checks the lines silently, storms up the gangway and into his cabin, and slams the door behind him. I get the story from Jay, and Ollie, veteran Chief of the Watch, who had taken the helm, and driven the ship the quarter mile across Nassau Harbor. Jay asked, "What else was I supposed to do?"

"I'll talk to the Captain. He doesn't want to see you now, and you don't want to see him."

The Old Man was livid, pacing around the cabin, trying to dispel his anger by walking, "If Ollie hadn't been here, I'd Court Martial Jay, bust his ass. What do you think I should do? No one moves my ship."

"Why don't we let things settle out? She's safely tied up. All is well. Let's get some dinner."

"Have the cook bring mine to the cabin."

Down below decks, Cromley is laughing and giving Jay shit, "Striking Captain, Matey?" He has taken Jay under his wings, they share that certain cockiness.

Jay's worried, rubs his chin in his hand.

Joe watches me and says nothing.

Wiz is also quiet, but for a different reason. Though Wiz was number one in his Academy class, the Old Man has always liked Jay better, not so academic, no intellectual. Wiz sees his status changing, he has climbed a notch on the ladder.

"Don't sweat it," I say, "You did what you felt you had to do. You have been certified as an Inport Officer of the Deck. This is what responsibility is all about."

"Am I going to Mast?"

"Relax. We need to let things settle out for a few days. The Captain will see you tomorrow. Just don't be so damn cocky."

"Nothing like a little excitement the first day in Nassau," Cromley pipes in, "let's go ashore. Conch fritters and a beer are sounding pretty good about now."

Again dutifully, I climb the ladder to the Cabin, knock, and poke my head in, "the EO and I are heading back out, want to come?"

The Old Man scowls. He won't leave his ship. His feet won't touch solid ground again until we return home to Mayport, three weeks hence.

WITCH DOCTOR

The boy, delirious, tossed about, cotton sheets unable to absorb the sweat. His temperature read nearly one-hundred-five degrees. He saw things we could not see, and spoke to beings that were not there. Or were they?

I paced the floor with worry. His mother washed his face with a cool washcloth. She had tried a cold water tub, yet still he suffered, nearly unconscious. She looked to me, and found no answer.

The fever had come on suddenly, and the tropical climate was foreign to us, transplanted northerners. Something in the humid air must have infected him. Or a bug, or the water. Maybe a snake, but he had no outward blemishes.

My son. So loving. My blond haired, three year old boy. He sat up straight in his bed, and looked through me toward the window into the pale light just past sunset. Momentarily lucid, he talked to the spirit being who stood behind me. Don't you see it, dad?

James talks incessantly, and demands direct attention. He sits in my lap, and if my attention wanes, grabs both my cheeks in his small hands, and forces me to meet his eyes.

I called the Mayport Naval Dispensary. A weekend, no doctors, bring him in Monday.

The Captain's wife, Iris, a Cuban recently arrived, she would know.

A few minutes later, we heard a knock on the door. A slight, dark-skinned woman entered without speaking. She carried a leather pouch. We led her to my son's room, where he lay motionless.

She reached into the pouch, and pulled out a small mason jar. From the jar, she removed a large pill, and placed the pill into my son's rectum. "El joven, Es' ok now."

Glenda had brewed coffee, and offered the woman a hand-thrown, pottery mug. She also gave the woman one of her prized mixing bowls. A gesture of thanks.

"Gracias." She wrote her name and phone number on a slip of paper, and walked out the door, leather pouch in hand.

KATY, KATY

"Watch it," Cromley yells over the drone of the chainsaw, "you'll cut your nuts off."

I'd flash him the finger, but would have to let go of the saw. Instead, I ponder the enormity of his offhand comment. I plan to keep my manhood. None of this cutting, no ceremonial slit. I've taken to this aura of fatherhood.

Glenda doesn't want any more children, after this one. Three will be enough, and all by Caesarian Section. Catholic upbringing or not, she'll have her tubes tied this go round.

A half-acre stand of scrub oak, and a few scraggly, jack pine mixed in, nothing like the hardwood forests back home in Michigan. Cromley knows the owner, and woke me early on a Saturday morning, "Let's go. I've got a case of beer, and gas and oil for the chainsaw. We can get enough fireplace wood for two years. Wear your boots."

Boots for the snakes. Water moccasins. Not much else lives in this north Florida island jungle, a lowland between the intercostal waterway and the Atlantic. A few Key deer, wild pigs, and snakes.

January, but still hot and humid, my shirt is soaked with sweat. We've been cutting wood all day. Cromley's rusty Mazda pickup, pushing two-hundred-fifty thousand miles, overflows with stacked firewood. I switch off the saw, limp toward the truck, pull the last two beers from the cooler, and toss one to Cromley. His muscled arm reaches out and catches the can in midair. He stands tall and strong in these woods, with a deep, burnt-on tan. He's the ship's Engineering Officer, a sailor all his life, and ten years my senior, though he works for me when we're on board the Cutter *Sweetgum*. Here, just friends, I call out, "Red on the head like a dick on a dog."

Cromley's young wife, younger than me, looks out the window, and watches while we stack his half of the wood. She's pretty, wants me to teach her the guitar. Cromley kids, laughs his belly laugh, "Ya, I know how that goes."

We figure we've sweated out the half case each, so stop off at the Anchor Bar for one last beer, before heading to my place to stack the last of the wood. By the time we leave, the sky has grown dark, and we can barely walk. Cromley drops me off without pulling into the drive, "I'll bring the wood over in the morning."

Glenda sits on the couch quietly. Elsa and James are already in bed, sleeping. I jump in the shower, dry off, and slump in a chair.

"I think I'm in labor. I've been having contractions all day."

She has my full attention. The appointment for the C-section is a week away. I call the doctor, "Get in here, now," she orders.

"I have to take a bath first, and wash my hair." And she does. My nervous fidgeting begins.

I call the neighbor to sit with the other, sleeping kids, start the VW Rabbit, and lay out a pillow and blanket in the passenger seat. She dries her thick, brown-black hair. Her contractions increase. I speed the twelve miles inland toward the hospital in Jacksonville, cross the bridge over the intercostal, and look down through the darkness. Deep black water turns into a jungle of scrub oak and pine. I swerve to dodge a small armored tank, an armadillo, feeding on a dead snake.

The doctor meets the car at the emergency drive-through entrance. Attendants help her onto a stretcher, and swoop her away. I park the car and run into the hospital.

Already in surgery. I wait, sober, no longer tired and worn from a day in the woods, no longer a drunken sailor on the town. And finally I hear, "You can see them now."

If we have a girl, we've decided, we'll call her Katy, Kathryn Elizabeth.

Katy, our third and youngest, clings to her mother's breast, and suckles urgently.

"I know I could have had her naturally," Glenda smiles, wistfully.

CHAPTER THREE

PART THREE – COMMAND AT SEA

I HEAR THE SEA IN THE WIND

I hear the sea
though a thousand miles
away
the wind blows
waving fields
of deep green barley
I feel the forgotten mist
salt in my hair
runs in my blood
I know the sound
cannot be the ocean
yet I hear the sea
in the wind

DEPARTURE

The Captain stood on the bridge wing as his polished crew of fifty souls performed the underway evolution like a dance troupe. Three years aboard the cutter, in command, and only now did he begin to understand the enormity of his responsibility. Only now, as the ship departed for a five-month deployment to the Caribbean, did he understand the heartache of leaving his family behind. A heartache he could not show to the crew. A heartache that would remain hidden through a Christmas season, and on past Easter, when god willing, he would return home to Charlevoix.

He had taken command as a relatively young officer, a rising star. Accolades abounded, for his work aboard previous ships, and on shore in administrative roles, where he served high-ranking decision-makers with distinction. He had graduated top of his class in graduate school at Monterrey. His future seemed limitless. He had been entrusted with command of a Coast Guard Cutter.

Many years ago, he had made a promise to himself. On a clear night, the lights of San Francisco twinkled, and blended, indistinguishable from the stars. He sat alone, on a bench in Dolores Park, and realized he must forge his own path, beholden to no one, man or woman. He was driven to the sea, caution be damned. And when the sea no longer held his dreams, he would know that, too.

The Captain reflected from the bridge of his ship, and wondered what he might try next. He chuckled at himself, knowing he was too old to play professional ball.

"Too smart," one salty veteran of several sea-going commands had chided him while pulling on a smoke, "you're too smart. But never mind me, I'm just an old sailor."

❧

He had sailed the cutter north to the American Soo shortly after taking command. The ship was scheduled for dry-dock maintenance at a contract facility that had never serviced a ship as large as the 180-foot Cutter *Mesquite*. A facility that had submitted the low bid.

Winds on the St. Mary's River gusted to thirty-five knots, making for a hard-working August day for the ship and crew. He watched as an experienced boatswains mate expertly conned the cutter alongside the moorings. The crew spent the night on the town. The young Captain walked the streets of the Soo, and greeted the young men enjoying liberty. He stopped for a single beer. He knew the coming morning's floating dry-dock evolution would require all his wits.

The ship's power plant had been dismantled at the dock in preparation for scheduled main engine work. A small, seemingly underpowered tug came alongside the stern, and the Captain took charge with only a bow-thruster for power assist. The steady current in the St. Mary's River carried the tug, and the ship's stern, downstream. Almost too far, he thought, as he envisioned the submerged dry dock escaping his outstretched grasp.

The Captain ordered the tug full ahead, and putting the bow-thruster stick full right, past the recommended stop, swung the bow quickly, and missed hitting the dry dock wall by a few feet. With the tug still pushing ahead, he reversed the thrust, and his ship settled safely into place.

Once moored in the dry dock, the contractor's crew took control of the ship. The Captain had an uncertain feeling about the shipyard manager, and handed the ship over reluctantly. He remained on the bridge to watch over the raising of the dry dock.

The yard workers attached eight steel cables to center the ship in the dry dock, while water was pumped from the submerged walls to create flotation. The Captain asked the manger if support timbers should also be positioned in place, in case the cables became strained?

"No. We don't need timbers until the ship is raised, then we'll build a cradle for the hull."

The Captain looked at the engineer from the Great Lakes support office in Cleveland, the expert, for guidance. The response in his eyes gave uneasy assurance.

As the dock began to rise, the ship began to lean.

As the ship leaned, the entire dry dock began to list.

A deafening, metallic ping, like a round from a cannon, pierced his ears.

A steel disc, ten inches in diameter, broke free of the dry dock wall, and shot as from a catapult into the super-structure of the ship. A second ping.

The Captain ordered all hands below deck immediately, looked the yard manager in the eyes, and ordered, "Put her down, now."

&

As his good ship departed the dock in Charlevoix, and floated easily in Round Lake, he placed his full concentration upon conning the cutter through the drawbridge, and out the Pine River Channel. Once the ship entered Lake Michigan, the steaming watch was set, and the crew settled in to a routine that would last the next five months.

A young seaman-apprentice walked about the decks with a manila envelope. Borrina, the short, stocky, and able Chief Bos'n, couldn't hold back a chuckle at the boot sailor who worried, "When do I pay the bridge toll?"

The Captain had lost a good deal of political capital when he had written a scathing letter to the Admiral in Cleveland that admonished the low-bid shipyard contract. A mid-level officer seldom criticizes his seniors. But he had taken the oath of command seriously, his ship came before his career, and he had gained the respect of his crew.

Alone in his cabin, he looked out the starboard side port-light to see Ile de Galets Lighthouse passing safely in the distance. He said a silent prayer for the safety of his family in his absence.

RULES OF THE ROAD

The track line took the ship through the Straits of Mackinac, thence down-bound in Lake Huron through a dark November evening. After twilight, he strolled about the bridge wing to identify stars, and welcomed the constellation Orion, one he quietly acknowledged as a good omen. Once they rounded Harrisville, and lost the lee of the Upper Peninsula of Michigan, rollers from the northeast helped the cutter make good time. The off duty men watched movies, read, ate, and slept, while a bridge watch of three souls guided the ship toward Port Huron.

The wind picked up from the west during the night, and the cutter rode in a trough of swells that had originated in Saginaw Bay. A dry run for the new folks, he thought, learning how to secure the ship for, and to live with, an unpredictable sea.

The Captain had planned the departure time to arrive at the entrance to the St. Clair River shortly after dawn. The confined river system would require his presence on the bridge for eight solid hours, while the cutter transited from Port Huron to Lake St. Clair, thence through Detroit to Toledo on the Detroit River.

❦

He recalled his first trip down the St. Clair River over two years earlier. A storm on Lake Huron had delayed their arrival at the river in Port Huron until nightfall. The young Captain had been apprehensive of the danger of travelling the narrow system in the dark, with only lighted navigational aids to guide him.

A couple miles into the river, they had passed a lighted buoy floating low in the water. And though it was dark, and the ship sailed in unfamiliar waters, he had come about, and fixed the buoy. The reliable Bos'n had welded the leak. He set the buoy back in the water using horizontal sextant angles, and left the aid watching properly. The evolution had taken several hours, and well past midnight, the crew had grown cold, tired, and a bit grumpy. Regardless, he could not pass by a navigational aid that needed to be serviced. A critical buoy that the master of a thousand-footer relied upon to transit the river.

The Captain reduced the bridge crew to allow the others to catch some sleep. His experienced Executive Officer took the con, but he remained watchful. The following current ran strong down-river, and assisted the ship. The Rules of the Road called for up-bound vessels to give way to down-bound. A ship can be better controlled driving into a current. Ships should also pass portside to portside whenever possible. And of course, this makes sense, like driving a car, stay to the right.

The lights of the St. Clair power plant came into view, and at the dock, he also noticed the mooring lights of a thousand-foot Great Lakes freighter. Over the radio, the freighter called to confirm a port-to-port passage. "This is the *Stuart J. Cort*, I'll be leaving the dock shortly, before you get here. Let's take it on one-whistle."

The XO answered, "Roger Cap, one-whistle."

The lights grew closer in the dark night. The thousand footer seemed to be fast to the dock. Another set of lights appeared, down river from the power plant. Another freighter made slow way, upbound toward Port Huron. The *Arthur M. Anderson* had made good time returning from Lake Erie.

The Cutter steamed rapidly downstream in the following current. The voice of the Captain of the *Cort* calmly rang out again over the radio, "I'm a going little slow here, *Mesquite*, better make it two-whistles."

The XO's eyes grew wide-open. He looked at the Captain, "I'm not comfortable here, can you take it?"

The Captain spoke clearly to the bridge crew, "I have the deck and con. XO, confirm two whistles with the *Cort*. And one whistle with the *Anderson*."

Firmly, to the helmsman, "Left standard rudder."

The *Cort* continued to pull away from the dock, but he knew that he must pass close aboard before he reversed the rudder to the right for a safe, one-whistle passage with the *Anderson*.

He found himself a kid, skiing a slalom course between monster ships, but this time instead of a ski edge, he had to control a two-thousand ton ship through two turns, in a following current.

Mesquite cleared the *Cort*, and was headed right at the *Anderson*. The radio crackled, "*Mesquite*, this is the *Anderson*, Cap, you gonna make it?"

He took the radio in hand, "Roger Cap, see you on one."

"Reverse your rudder to right-standard."

When the two ships had passed at a safe distance, he announced, "XO has the deck and con," and returned the XO's salute.

He walked to the bridge wing, extended his arms, and waved to the Captain of the *Anderson*, the last ship to have seen the Fitzgerald afloat.

The wave was returned, and the radio crackled, "Nice work, Captain."

⋙

The cutter sailed beneath the Blue Water Bridge shortly after dawn. A new, inexperienced Executive Officer, Lt. Phil Smiley, met him on the bridge, and relieved the Officer of the Deck. The river was clear of traffic, and sparkled blue in the November sunlight. The Captain quizzed Phil over the Rules of the Road, " Which is the burdened vessel in the St. Clair River, up-bound or down-bound?"

"Up-bound," the XO replied.

The Captain grinned, "How about the law of gross tonnage?"

His family back home faded into the hidden reaches of his mind. His ship and crew became his primary concern, according to the Rules of the Road.

ONTARIO

The aging, mammoth-sized doors of the triple lock in the Welland Canal loomed nearly one hundred feet above his ship. He could not help but think what might happen should any one of the lock doors fail. The cutter might ride the resulting torrent of fresh water, or she might topple and turn, and be carried under.

A "salty" sat in the top lock basin, and floated like a mirage. He wondered at the magic of engineering that had created this lock system many years ago. He wondered how long before some critical element failed.

The only route for large ships to avoid the Niagara River, and the majestic falls, the Welland is a twenty-six mile canal through southern Ontario. In the space of those twenty-six miles, water drops three hundred twenty-six feet toward sea level. The salty, an ocean-going freighter, would pass the cutter once they reached Lake Ontario, in a hurry to clear the St. Lawrence for the Atlantic Ocean before the system closed for the winter. A closing dependent upon weather.

The cutter shared a deadline with the salty, but the Captain, confident in his reinforced, icebreaking hull, had planned the trip with several, purposeful, overnight stops along the way. To refresh the crew, to make this trip to the Caribbean an adventure they would never forget, and to give them time to set aside longings for loved ones waiting back home.

The ship left the Welland Canal, entered Lake Ontario, and anchored off the Niagara Bar for some deserved rest at 2:30 am.

Underway again at dawn, he worked two buoys before turning east toward Niagara, an American hamlet that lay inside the mouth of the Niagara River. Fort Niagara towered on a hill, and overlooked the river mouth. A ten-knot current, created by the Falls, ran for more than ten miles down the river. Dangerous, swirling eddies carried well out into the calm lake.

❧

He was used to operating in currents. He had cut his teeth on the tidal flows of the Kuskoquim River, and False Pass in Alaska. And tidal current became a constant friend during his time on the St. John's River, in northern Florida. Most fresh water sailors understood the wind's effect on navigation, but had not operated in heavy currents.

The Captain recalled his first buoy operation aboard *Mesquite*, three years earlier, when he rode the ship on a familiarization cruise before taking command. He conned the ship toward an open water buoy, on a calm Lake Michigan day. He had powered the ship opposite the buoy, set the bow across what he believed to be a current, and waited for the natural force to bring the buoy close to the deck, and near his prospective crew, waiting below.

He waited, patiently.

He waited, and the crew grew restless, and looked up toward the bridge.

Following an extended, pregnant pause, he powered the bow close to the buoy, and completed the operation. "Cautious but safe," the Commander he would be relieving had commented, " I see a man who has operated in current."

The Captain knew he had much to learn about the Great Lakes.

∂

He set the bow across the strong Niagara current, and waited patiently as the flow eased the ship alongside the dock at Station Niagara. Liberty was piped for all but the in-port duty section, and the men headed for the closest watering hole.

The Captain took a solitary hike ashore to stretch his legs. He looked down over the river mouth from the heights of the Fort, which had been built in the early 1700's, before the French and Indian War. He looked down over his cutter, detached, as he might view a painting, a print of a ship floating in the snug, pastoral setting of a winter harbor. Yet he knew that pictures never tell the whole story.

SEA SMOKE

The eastern end of Lake Ontario lay out before him enveloped in an eerie shroud. Bitter cold temperatures had descended from Canada overnight, and had failed to blend with the still-warm lake water. A layer of pure white, frozen fog hung suspended. From the sunny, bitter-cold bridge, at a height of thirty-seven feet, the Captain looked down over a thick carpet that hid landmarks, rock outcroppings, and a floating, lighted, red bell buoy.

The previous evening, as the cutter entered Oswego Harbor to spend the night, he had received a radio message to call the operations boss back in Cleveland. He found a phone in a sailor's bar, having walked the few blocks from the docks with Chief Bodie Noble, the guy on the ship that he trusted to keep the engines running. Bodie, the same age, and having served on several tenders previously, had become his sounding board, and his confidant.

"I need you to remove eight more buoys around Stony Island on your way to the St. Lawrence. I know you are in a time crunch, but this will save the *Mariposa* a trip through the locks," the four-striper had relayed.

"Aye-aye, sir."

She was a hard-working ship. He had worked more navigational aids than any of the other four cutters in the Lakes during his three-year tour in command. Yet he felt like a step-child. The other cutters were commanded by Academy men. The bosses in Cleveland were Academy. He was a Mustang officer, a man who knew what it was like to take orders, and to salute someone for whom he had lost respect.

But he took solace in the little things, in seemingly minor interactions with individual crewmen, in the compliments on his carriage, and in keeping them safe. He reveled in the unspoken messages received from the natural world, a calm sunset over an endless horizon, a well-planned evolution, the twinkling lights in a harbor left safe for the passage of a ship and captain he would never know. He sat at this bar in Oswego, and recalled the eyes of the barmaid in St. Ignace who served drinks to the crews of all the Lakes' cutters. She had spotted him a beer, to wash down that State Bar burger he relished after a long autumn day working on the northern Lake Michigan, "I hear that Captain of the *Mesquite* is the best."

Selling this trip to the Caribbean, to the crew he cared for like a family, had not been easy. The single men, and his younger single officers, two men, and two young women, both top-notch Academy graduates, had chomped at the bit for the adventure. He knew that even the more senior, married men secretly looked forward to the trip of a career, to the warm, southern waters. But in a family-sized crew of fifty, one dissenter can foment trouble.

Bodie's boss had been aboard since August. The Captain felt a mate's allegiance to Jack, who had overseen Bodie's repair of a cracked engine block in one of the main engines at a critical time, during Refresher Training. The ship had failed in the Captain's first training exercise a year earlier because of the engine. The Captain's boss at the time had been frank, no veiled threat, "you have to make it through next year."

Returning a year later, with a brand new crew, the ship had performed admirably, and gained accolades, the block "E," for "Excellent" that adorned the superstructure.

Jack had lost any fervor to serve. He had taken his orders to the cutter in order to retire in the small, picturesque town of Charlevoix. But he had time to go before he would become eligible, and had "retired on active duty." He bellyached about the trip to anyone who would listen.

Jack made his lack of respect for Phil, the Executive Officer, plain. He had grown up in the "old Guard," before women went to sea, and carried a grudge toward the two young women officers. He especially disliked LTJG Cassidy, the Operations Officer, third-in-line, and senior to Jack. The Captain had taken Cassidy under his wing, though the capable young woman, a top Academy graduate, could surely handle herself. He remembered how Captain Black had protected him so many years ago on the Bering Sea, when he conflicted with crusty old Bos'n Stubbs. Some personalities will never mix.

The Captain had seen the symptom before. In his three years, he had received several similar crew assignments. Guys who had been around, who knew the assigning officer, and wanted a cushy, comfortable job to end their careers.

But the Captain maintained his inherent stoicism. He hadn't complained to superiors. He believed in finding a peaceful solution, and had grown weary of politics. He lifted responsibility upon his big shoulders, never asked for help. He knew this would be his last shipboard duty, that before too long, he would walk down the brow for good.

Silent and solitary, and never a complainer, the Captain played the hand he had been dealt.

Time crunch, he muttered to himself. That desk jockey in Cleveland has no idea. He nestled up to the bar for a beer before returning to the ship to set sailing orders for dawn.

❧

Standing on the bridge-wing in below zero cold, he heard the ringing of the bell before the forward lookout spotted the red buoy. He eased the cutter alongside, and Chief Bos'n Borrina, another trusted friend, lifted the buoy with the boom. The deck crew quickly changed out the lighted buoy for a winter marker that would float under the ice, until spring.

On December tenth, with eight buoys on deck, the cutter entered the St. Lawrence River through sea smoke off Cape Vincent. Dark had long since fallen. He had hoped to moor in Clayton, New York, to unload the buoys, and rest in preparation for the three-day trip downriver to Quebec City.

But the dock in Clayton appeared a tattered mess of pilings, surely unable to hold the cutter. Cold, and tired from a full day on the bridge, the Captain set the anchor in view of the dull lights of the small town. He nestled in his rack, and slept like a baby, until dawn.

A THOUSAND ISLANDS

As in a river-scape captured within a glass ball, light snowflakes fell around the ship. From time to time, the snow stopped , and a ray of sun burst through the clouds. Stone castles and wooden cottages lined the shore, where the currents had not etched rock into cliffs. Ship-channels narrowed through cuts between a myriad of deep, green islands. One after another, the islands never seemed to end. The flow took the ship ever down-river, toward the sea.

Shortly after their dawn departure from anchor, the sea smoke had dissipated. Like a fairy-land, he thought to himself. A place to return to, in another life.

◌

The cutter encountered the first significant ice of the season in the pool downstream of the Eisenhower Lock. The familiar sound of ice scraping against the steel hull would travel with them for a while.

The deck crew scurried small chunks away from the concrete wall, and he eased the ship into the Snell lock. Finally, a pier where he could unload the buoys, and prepare for sea.

The cutter departed the lock, left the United States, and entered Canadian waters with a clear, clean deck. The mood on the ship soared with a positive beat. More than the buoys, more than the Great Lakes, had been left in the ship's wake.

QUEBEC

Through the windows of the gondola, he looked out at the snow-capped Laurentians. Skiing presents a singular purpose, and requires complete concentration. The skier is transported from mundane cares, and carried into the mountain world.

❧

A harbor pilot had come aboard, and guided the ship into Montreal, where two new pilots boarded together. Why two, he wondered? I could safely navigate this river without a pilot's assistance, but would risk an international incident. Canadian laws protect jobs on their soil, and in their waters.

The Captain enjoyed the repartee with these admirable individuals, eccentric to the man, and professional. The lead pilot in Montreal lithely climbed the rope ladder from the pilot boat, and swung on to the cutter's deck. He dressed like a movie star, with shiny black shoes beneath black, pressed wool slacks. Under an expensive, knee-length, leather top coat, he wore a white turtleneck sweater against the cold night.

The Captain had studied French in college, and surprised the pilot, who could manage only broken English. The second man was in training, and stood in the back of the bridge, out of the way.

Each pilot had a small section of the river to memorize. Another had been called to meet the ship in Trois Riviere – Three Rivers. The Captain was sorry to see the movie star depart, and even sorrier when the oncoming pilot was delayed well into the wee hours of the morning.

While waiting for the pilot boat, the cutter encountered fairly thick ice in the harbor. White sheets began to raft in the constant current. The Captain watched while a salty, also awaiting a pilot, ran engines full ahead into the current and ice, and began to drag anchor toward a highway bridge. Over the radio, he heard a plea, "Pilot, Vite! Vite!"

A pair of harbor tugs responded toward the salty, and behind the tugs, the pilot boat came into view heading to the cutter. The ice had formed early this year. Some ships might not make the sea before the river closed.

The City of Quebec stood high on a granite outcropping. The ancient French fort, built to protect the city from all directions, overlooked the St. Lawrence River. He moored the ship at a downtown dock just before noon. They would stay two nights, to rest and relax before striking out to sea. The Captain took a shuttle to the Laurentian Mountains.

❦

He set his ski tips high as the gondola arrived at the crest of the mountain. He pushed off, and glided to a stop. He looked out at the rocky-snow expanse, and in the distance, the icy St. Lawrence River flowed, through the Charlevoix Region of Quebec, ever to the sea.

AROUND THE GASPE

The Captain looked forward to seeing Halifax again. He and his wife had travelled there, fifteen years earlier, before OCS, before kids, before responsibility had overtaken their freestyle lives.

The cutter departed the dock from Quebec City promptly at eight hundred hours with a harbor pilot on board who had expected a warm breakfast waiting. "Might not make it out," he said gruffly, "too much ice, too thick, two feet. No more boats."

"We're going," the Captain replied, pointed east, and picked up the radio handset.

"Canadian Icebreaker *Radisson*, this is the United States Coast Guard Cutter *Mesquite*. Cap, we could use a little help here."

He felt the ominous distinction of being the last ship to depart the St. Lawrence River for the season. From here on out, they would be alone.

"Thanks *Radisson*. We'll see you in the spring."

⚓

The cutter made eleven knots good all day long in a following, downriver current. They had out-sailed the flowing, freshwater ice. He had read the forecast for a westerly gale, and hoped the wind would provide a following sea for the transit around the Gaspe Peninsula.

Just before dark, the helmsman lost control of the ship's wheel. The rudder would not respond. "General Quarters" sounded throughout the cutter. The crew took their stations. The Captain rushed to after-steering in the stern of the ship, to check the steering motor. On the way, he heard the pipe, "Stand down from drill, resume normal steaming watch."

He boiled inside, and called the XO to report to his cabin. Jack, along with Phil, responsible for ship's training, had disengaged the steering motor. "A test for the crew," Phil reported, before the Captain rebuked him, only half-calm. "Never without my permission."

Moments later, Jack appeared at the cabin door, his eyes wild. "Yell at me, not the XO," he spouted.

He had lost any surviving confidence in Jack. He took a deep breath.

Fortunately in Bodie, he had an engineer on board in whom he could place his trust. He had always told himself, and believed, give me a good engineer, and I can take a ship anywhere.

And Phil. He had no confidence in the XO. Phil would never be a Captain. Fortunately, in his junior officers, and in the other senior enlisted men, he had a crew that could be trusted.

"Never without my permission," he repeated, firmly.

∝

A following sea took the ship around the Gaspe Peninsula at a healthy twelve knots. After rounding Cap de Rosiers, a significant ground swell hit from the southwest, and put the ship in the trough on their intended southeast track. The Captain tacked the cutter four times during the night to provide a quartering sea.

On the short, southwest leg, required to clear Ile de la Madelaine, six foot swells began to hit the bow, and freeze on impact. He worried about the weight of the ice on the superstructure. Too much weight could destroy the delicate balance of flotation, and cause the ship to capsize. He had sailed in the Bering, and dealt with more significant ice build-ups, but breathed much easier after the final turn, downwind, toward the Strait of Canso.

The Strait cuts through eastern Nova Scotia, and saves vessels a several-hundred mile trip out and around the island. One lock separates the Gulf of St. Lawrence from the Atlantic Ocean. The ship passed through the lock, changed three feet in elevation, and entered the North Atlantic. A pink sunset, and a pod of whales greeted their turn west toward Halifax.

A fast moving low passed during the night, and brought forty-knot winds first from the east, before backing to the northwest. Conditions became too rough to transfer a pilot. Rather, the Captain followed the pilot boat into Halifax Harbor.

He moored the cutter alongside the Canadian destroyer Saguenay, the first Canadian warship he had ever seen. Several Canadian submarines, old World War II vintage, flanked the destroyer, to save on limited pier space.

The Captain, and his officers, along with the senior Chiefs, dined aboard the Saguenay, and enjoyed cocktails and wine with fresh salmon. Very civilized, he thought to himself. Jack stayed in his stateroom, and sulked like a spoiled child.

No alcohol is allowed aboard a Coast Guard Cutter. Probably a good rule in the long run, he thought. He recalled enjoying cocktails on the fantail of the Cutter Mackinaw, while in port in Chicago, the night before the Chicago to Mackinac sailboat race. He had shared a conversation with a tipsy Paul Harvey, and learned the rest of the story.

And in Alaska, many years ago, aboard the *Ironwood*, Captain Black had carried cases of Olympia in the reefers, and on rare occasions, allowed the off-duty crew two beers each. Of course, trades had been made, and a few bad apples imbibed more than they could handle. Probably a good rule, he thought.

Mesquite remained moored in Halifax the next day and night. Christmas was in the air. Lights sparkled and fir trees shone from every townhouse window. Many of the crew toured the old city, but the young men found the staid Canadian nightlife lacking.

The Captain began to realize that he would miss Christmas with his family for the first time. He shook those thoughts loose from his head, and focused on the coming, seven-day trip in the open, North Atlantic Ocean.

CAPTAIN'S LOG
TOWARD WARM WATERS

Departed Halifax on the morning of the 19th for Savannah, Georgia, and our Christmas celebration. Steering two-two-four degrees true — one course will take us around Cape Hatteras to the Savannah River entrance – eleven-hundred and fifty nautical miles. We will pass eighty nautical miles to the east of Cape Cod in our closest approach to land.

Encountered our first fishing fleet. A new maneuvering experience for the young officers who have been weaned on the Great Lakes. Another whale sighting, close aboard, and passing within thirty yards. A Blue whale, I think.

December 20th — Carrying ever on. Winds picked up above thirty knots during the evening. Seas built to twelve feet, and hit us head on through the night. Made only eight knots good.

The winter solstice arrived during the night, at 0800 Greenwich Mean Time. The maximum angle of declination of the sun below the celestial equator. Morning will bring the shortest day.

December 21st — Underway in the North Atlantic. Encountered the Gulf Stream current. Even with the seas subsiding, we have difficulty making nine knots good.

Sea water temperatures rose twenty degrees, into the seventies Fahrenheit. On schedule to make Savannah by Christmas Eve. On this Solstice, we have seen the last of our true northern winter.

December 22nd — Another day at sea. The sun finally came out today, accompanied by a warm, southerly breeze to air us all out. Off-duty crew members relax above decks in the sun.

A wind shift to the north created a four-foot quartering sea, making a bar-b-que and the crew's "No Talent" night a rousing success. Who knew we had such creative minds aboard? Folks will surprise you when you get to know them.

––––––––––––––   ––––––––––––––

December 23rd — Around Cape Hatteras at 2000 hours. Will arrive Savannah on the morning of Christmas Eve.

––––––––––––––   ––––––––––––––

December 24th & 25th, 1988 — Entered the Savannah River at 0800, moored to the City waterfront pier by 1000. Sunny and seventy degrees, shorts and T-shirts. Shoppers abound, finishing up last minute items.

The Morale Committee held a Christmas party for the crew. We had stowed away gifts from loved ones back home as a surprise. Quiet appreciation. Bittersweet.

Attended evening candlelight services with a few of the officers. Exercised with a brisk walking tour through old Savannah on Christmas Day. Somehow the warmth and sunshine help to mitigate feelings of being away from home for the holidays.

Is Christmas always like this in the South?

BAHAMAS

He laid out a cast, and watched the reflection of the silver and blue spoon gently float to a fifty foot bottom, like a leaf falling from a tree. Suddenly, a tug hit, the line tightened, and he was transported back in time. A tow-headed blond boy hauled in a channel cat on the Chesapeake Bay.

He saw his son on the pier in Monterrey. James, then a boy of five years, intent on the mackerel as his father reeled the fish. The look of wonder in James' eyes at lunch on the wharf, with squid, prepared like manicotti in a garlic marinara.

He had introduced the boy to trout fishing a year later while they camped near Bryce Canyon. A clear, rocky stream tumbled down from mountain heights.

The Captain hauled in a spotted grouper, two feet long, tossed the fish back, and cast again.

Perhaps that was the moment when he decided to retire from the sea. He missed his son, and his wife, and the darling girls. The sea had given him a good life, yet had taken so much.

⚓

Mesquite had sailed from Miami on the New Year. He had never served in the law-enforcement arm of the Guard, and approached the work with trepidation. They had loaded two Rigid-hull inflatable boats, nicknamed "Hurricanes," on the buoy deck. The boats, with Volvo inboard-outboard engines, ran like the wind. The crew had been trained, and the young officers had been qualified, to board vessels suspected of illegal activities. Young sailors armed with automatic weapons, he mused.

The first night out, they had crossed the Straits of Florida, and gone to anchor off the Little Bahamas Bank. The fishing lamp had been lit, and to any passing vessel, the ship posed as if enjoying a recreational trip. But up on the bridge, the operations officer kept a sharp radar watch on any traffic in the area. Many of the crew fished, and the cook made a meal of the catch.

Once darkness fell, the order went out to darken ship, and the Captain weighed anchor. Like a police cruiser hidden around the next curve, the cutter might suddenly appear, followed by a call on the radio, "This is the United States Coast Guard, halt, and prepare to be boarded."

Cocaine cowboys ruled the Caribbean. Their fast-boats could outrun the fastest Hurricane. If ever cornered, the hired guns could scuttle the drug lord's half-million dollar fast-boat, along with the illegal cargo, in deep water. Once the boat was gone to the depths, the cowboys called for help, and the mission turned into a rescue. A month later, they would be back, with a new boat, and fresh cargo.

The Captain saw the futility of the mission, but saluted and carried on. Most of the crew wondered why they had been sent so far from home.

Fishing, or swim calls, filled the daily routine, and through the night the cutter patrolled. But the waters were hypnotizing. Shades of blue and green sparkled in unending sunlight. Fresh fish became the menu staple.

Officers from the Royal Bahamian Defense Force embarked in Nassau, to formalize the boardings. The legalities became tricky. A US cutter might board a Venezuelan or Columbian boat, in Bahamian waters. Many of the surrounding governments did not support, and in fact, ignored American efforts to stop the drug trade at the source. Cuban waters were to be avoided at all costs.

Mesquite ran for ten-day periods between official port calls to refuel and take on fresh water. They would rendezvous with smaller cutters, and offload fuel and water, like a mother ship.

Life was slow, and too easy. An anchorage in the Pelican Cays, in 150 feet of water, and the anchor sat on the bottom, magnified as if through a lens. A trip around Eleuthera Island, toward Exuma, and a meeting with the Cutter *Manitou*, named for an island back home in Lake Michigan. Thoughts of home, and the Captain's favorite trip, to the Manitou Islands, the bear cubs, lost in the lake, while mother bear lay asleep. Monumental sand dunes left in the wake of her slumber.

On a Sunday holiday, at anchor off Little San Salvador, they cooked burgers on a grill. The crew played on the sandy shore, swam, and snorkeled along the coral reefs that line the island, not far from where Columbus first landed. An uninhabited paradise, a day at the beach.

Liberty call in Nassau. He watched the tourists and the thieves at the straw market. The bustling humanity in the warm, humid sunshine. He refreshed with an ocean swim. The salt dried, and caked on his fair skin. He won ten dollars at blackjack, but lost it all, except a quarter, for the pay phone, to call home.

Back on board, the Captain received a radio message from the operations center in Miami. Sail at first light. Return to Miami for supplies. Prepare for operations in Puerto Rico, and the U.S. Virgin Islands.

CAPTAIN'S LOG
THE VIRGINS

January 12th — Underway from Nassau enroute Miami for water, fuel, and supplies. Sailing with a light ship, stability lacking, and feels like it.

Lieutenant JG Keith Bills, our talented mustang officer, and the son of a Navy submarine captain, had missed the trip south for medical leave. Fortunately, he met the ship in Miami. His mother, re-married to a retired British Royal Navy Officer, lived on the beach in Nassau, and hosted the entire crew for a memorable cookout.

One man missed morning movement. The young buck was last seen in a bar with two college girls. Told them he was on the cruise ships. Hope he is alright, Nassau can be a tough town.

Arrived Miami after midnight. Made ready for the trip to Puerto Rico. Caught a few hours rest.

January 14th -17th — Departed Miami at 0900 bound for Puerto Rico, a four-day journey. Sailed generally east to avoid the Gulf Stream, and to find the lee of the Grand Bahama Bank for the turn south. Tomorrow we will make the Old Bahama Channel, a stone's throw from Cuba.

Passed through the Old Bahama Channel. Seas built as we lost our lee to the north and east. A rather non-descript day on the ocean. Sunday, like a listless, lazy Sunday back home. I miss the Detroit Free Press.

The Captain of the Cutter *Vigorous*, a 210 foot law enforcement ship, requested rendezvous for underway replenishment. Why does a ship with evaporators need water from one that cannot make fresh water? Pulling rank, methinks. The crew sees things plain. Jack complains, but this time he is right. Aye-aye, Sir.

Around Great Inagua Island, steaming north of Haiti. Slow, steady progress while beating into the easterlies, and an ever-present, brisk, twenty-five knot wind.

January 18th — Arrived San Juan Harbor at sunset. The Old Fort towers above the dirty city, and guards all approaches. Caught a touch of the flu, or maybe I'm feeling the effects of drinking Florida water stored in the ship's tanks. The metallic taste invades our lives, the odor present even in our clothes. A few days' rest, a walking tour of the fort, and a rum punch will do fine, thank you.

———————   ———————

January 23rd — Left Old San Juan as the morning waned. Turned further east, again into the constant trade winds. Our destination, to patrol the Virgins, south of St. John Island. These waters were once the dominion of the Cutter *Sagebrush*, decommissioned two years ago. Her motto, "We Serve the Virgins."

Apparently the Virgins were too much for her. I look at our cutter's plaque with pride, "Workhorse of the Great Lakes.

———————   ———————

January 24th — Commenced twenty-four hour a day patrol coverage. A coordinated evolution, with eight other cutters involved. A high intensity blockade of the U.S. Virgin Islands.

Beautiful scenery — hills, multi-colored water, white sails, haciendas on the overlooks. Anchored off Canal Bay, near the United Kingdom's territorial boundary. Lousy fishing, but a good night's sleep.

Conducted boardings through the morning. The coordinated operation made one significant bust. Bails of cocaine on the bridge of a Liberian-registered freighter. We had tracked the ship on radar. Another cutter made the seizure. Fortunately no gun play.

Swim call in clear, deep water. The Gunner's Mate stands on the bow, M-16 rifle at the ready. He watches for sharks.

———————   ———————

January 26th — Underway from anchor while the sun rises over the British Virgins. Entered St. Thomas harbor in shallow water. Mud churned fore and aft. Rough town off main street. Too many fruity, rum punches, made with Crucian brand. Chastised by a few of the crew for walking back to the ship alone.

———————   ———————

January 27th — January 31st

Left Charlotte Amalie, St. Thomas Island, with the noon tide, bound for San Juan.

Resupplied water and perishable food after arrival near sunset.

Departed San Juan at 0800 into a northerly ground swell. Should catch a lee from the eastern-most Bahamas later this evening. Wind shifted to the east, finally. Still rolling, but a following-sea roll now. Making twelve knots good.

General malaise set in. Too much time off, not enough to do. No ship traffic sighted. Long watches, electronic fixes.

Arrived Miami for our ten-day, mid-deployment break. The family men will receive a round-trip plane flight home.

Since departing Charlevoix, we have steamed seventy-four hundred and fourteen Nautical Miles.

CRAB RACES

The off-duty crew gathered at the Wreck, a sailor's bar that overlooks the harbor in Christiansted, St. Croix. A barefooted folksinger kept beat on a wooden plank floor. His heel pounded louder than a base drum. The Captain put a ten-spot on a luminescent-green crab, and awaited the gun.

Earlier in the day, the ship had serviced the sea buoy that marked the harbor entrance. The channel into Christiansted wound through a myriad of coral reefs in unpredictable S-curves. He had put the small boat over to sound the bottom with a lead line, and he had studied the Harbor Pilot, a book that described the entry in detail. The best advice he had gleaned, warned, read the water color.

So many shades of blue and green presented themselves, as the bottom of the sea drew closer to the surface, before dropping away once again.

⚮

February was coming to a close, and by the Ides of March, the cutter would be released to return to the Lakes.

The Captain had flown home for a too-short week to see his family. He skied with the kids on the small town hill, Mount McSauba, and wore out his gloves on the tow rope. He recalled looking down at Lake Michigan and Grand Traverse Bay from the window of the small plane. Colors so similar to these Caribbean blues and greens, yet it was sand, not coral, that shaded the depths in his fresh water home.

⚮

Back and forth, up and down, like a yoyo in the hands of a faceless monarch. The command in Miami used the ship like a rental car, without care for the crew.

Following the break, the cutter had resumed law-enforcement work in the Bahamas. Even the almost daily fishing calls had become monotonous. Yet he found himself mesmerized by the beauty of their surroundings, places where he had anchored in fifty feet of clear ocean, and on the swing, the ship had crossed a bank where the bottom lay a mile straight down.

He had caught a trigger fish of blue, silver, and green, like a large specimen from a parlor fish tank. Off Green Cay, the crew cast into a school of three-foot Mako sharks on the edge of a six-hundred fathom bank. A few had been kept, and battered to kill, before razor-sharp teeth could reach a mark. Most thrown back to the sea. Riding the anchor near a deserted island beach, the cook roasted tasty filets over an open fire. A taste much like sirloin beef.

Mid-month, the puppeteer sent sailing orders to return to San Juan to repair buoy discrepancies. Another thousand miles east into the trade winds, but at least they travelled for a solid reason, to do the work the ship did best.

The Captain had anchored off Little San Salvador, to swim, cook the mid-day meal, and wait out a lessening of the wind. Relative calm arrived in the evening. During the following four-day beat into the seas, sparse company was provided by whales, and acrobatic flying fish. Occasionally, a fish flew over the bow, and lay marooned on deck.

Old and well past its prime, with parts hard to come by, the ship's power plant acted up again. In the lee of deep swells, he had shut down both main engines for servicing, and kept the ship's head into the seas with the bow thruster. Jack burst onto the bridge, worried, "Captain, we'll have to turn back to Miami for parts."

The Captain harbored doubts concerning Jack's advice. What motivations lay hidden beneath the conversation? He placed his confidence in Bodie, and the other senior enlisted men.

"We're more than halfway to San Juan. Do all you can, jury-rig as needed, we will carry on."

After a few hours delay, the cutter pushed east, running on one engine. Another hour, and the second engine came on line. He sent an urgent message to Miami for new parts to be airlifted to San Juan. The garbled response, "We have a routine scheduled flight next week."

The cutter spent a week in Puerto Rico, cleaned up the San Juan harbor buoys, and ventured along the north shore to service buoys in other small,

Puerto Rican sea towns. Still running on oft-repaired cams, he stayed close to San Juan, while waiting for parts to arrive.

⚓

The Captain considered that the sea gods had looked down with good fortune on *Mesquite*. Hoisting tons of steel buoys onto a rocking platform is inherently dangerous work. The Captain routinely placed the ship in danger to accomplish the mission. Rocky shoals that are marked by buoys lay only a failed engine away.

And he admired his well-trained buoy deck crew. He constantly oversaw their safety. He carried pride in the fact that his crew ran injury free throughout his time in command. Ever vigilant, he thought, ever vigilant. Bring them home safely.

⚓

After a long day working in San Juan harbor, he and a few officers had walked uptown into Old San Juan for drinks and a seafood dinner. Afterwards, most remained in town, while he and the Operations Officer headed back to the ship to check on the status of repairs. The parts had finally arrived. He was anxious to depart Puerto Rico for good.

They walked down a narrow, alley-like street toward the moorings. Two shapes, a young man and woman, eased off a stone wall, and followed them. Suddenly, two young Hispanic men leapt from a doorway. One grabbed the Captain, who stood taller and stronger than his assailant, and he shoved the lighter man away. The man regrouped, and pointed to his partners, who held LTJG Cassidy by both arms, and brandished a knife.

The Captain raised his arms, "Here, take my cash, almost fifty dollars."

His assailant reached into the Captain's pockets, and pulled out a small, scrimshaw pocket knife. "Please, don't take that. It was a gift from my wife."

The young woman grabbed the knife, and the cash from the Captain's wallet. Four shapes disappeared into the dark, humid night.

The Captain turned back toward the tourist section of town, and found a policeman walking the street. The cop shrugged, as if to say, "this happens all the time. Let it go, go on home"

He ground his teeth, and his temper began to swirl. Incredulous, he saw himself wandering through the end of the movie "Chinatown." A crowd swirled in, and buried any trace of mishap.

❧

He bought the folksinger a drink. During the monologue, LTJG Bills had discovered that the singer spent his summers entertaining at the Shamrock, a bar on Beaver Island, twenty Lake Michigan miles from their Charlevoix home. He wondered at the strength of the man's bare heel, his continual stomping on wooden planks, sounding a steady beat.

The Captain lost ten bucks on the greenish crab, and walked back to the ship, safely in a crowd of happy sailors.

CAPTAIN'S LOG
DRY TORTUGAS

February 28th — Departed Christiansted at 0900. Following wind and seas made for a pleasant journey west.

Mid-afternoon, I received a call from San Juan, a buoy sinking in the channel near St. Thomas, can you respond? Of course, come about, now into the seas. A six-hour trip back will cost us a day's liberty in Key West.

Fixed the buoy at midnight. A good, professional effort by the crew working late, after dark, in unfamiliar waters. Westbound once again. Destination Key West.

Sailed north of Puerto Rico, finally, I hope, leaving San Juan off the port quarter. Surfing with the trade-winds, and following, twenty-five foot swells.

March 2nd — Continue enroute Key West. No ship traffic, and occasional glimpses of land.

Avoided a potentially serious problem with the port main diesel engine. A set screw had worked loose, fortunately the watch heard a noise, and shut down. Might have had a cam-follower through the engine block. Repaired, and on our way.

Entered the Old Bahama Channel, again a stone's throw from Cuban waters. Vigilance to our position fixes.

March 4th — Arrived at the Key West sea buoy at midnight. Entry waylaid by Miami asking us to board a suspicious Panamian freighter. Released upon reporting a troublesome pneudyne system. Unable to control the propeller revolutions on the bridge.

Like the old days, I conned the cutter to the dock by relaying commands to Jack in the engine room. Safely moored.

March 5th – 9th — In port Key West for liberty. Beaches, above-ground cemeteries, and swimming in the luxurious pool at the Navy Officer's Club.

Sought out Jack for a man to man talk. Over a beer, I confided my two experiences at Captain's Mast as an enlisted man. Once for an Unauthorized Absence when I returned late for muster after having considered going AWOL, but thought better.

The second time I was charged for not reporting a fellow sailor's misdeed, and stood silent before the Old Man. One hand for yourself, the other for ship and crew.

Jack finally decided to confide in me, and opened up. Family troubles called him home. His misogynistic attitudes toward the women officers also became startlingly clear. I searched for a peaceful, middle ground. I could not defend his demoralizing comments, yet felt a loyalty to him as a shipmate, and wanted to help.

Jack was a troubled soul who pounded a bible, yet apparently failed to read the book. He asked for leave to return home early. If granted, he would miss the trip back through Canada. The ship might be better without him. I grow tired of the drama.

The final night in port, I painted the town with Bodie, the next engineer in line. We finished the night listening to Billy Joel covers by a pop-folksinger, and in our inebriated state, purchased his cassette. I trusted Bodie, and his judgement. He could handle the engineering duties should I send Jack home.

I pitched the cassette over the side on our morning departure.

March 9th — Left Key West for Florida Bay, north of the Keys, to conduct fisheries patrol. We will be looking for poachers who net shrimp inside the Sanctuary breeding grounds.

March 10th — Underway in Florida Bay, the Gulf of Mexico, conducting Federal Shrimp Sanctuary boundary patrol. Just before midnight, observed several shrimp boats apparently trawling within the sanctuary. Launched the Hurricane, but we were unable to actually observe nets down, and nine foot swells precluded boarding. All of the observed vessels "hightailed it" out of the protected zone.

Our presence stopped the poaching, even though we didn't catch them. Made for the Dry Tortugas, and a lee anchorage.

March 11th — Anchored off Dry Tortuga, with the Fort Jefferson National Monument in sight. Discovered a forty foot crab boat hard aground in the harbor. Crew claimed they had been there for five days, unable to raise assistance. I dropped our motor-cargo boat, and the crew tried to pull her off the rocks. No luck – will try again at high tide.

Tortugas – "Turtles" so named by Ponce de Leon. "Dry" as a bone. No fresh water.

The Fishing Vessel Cooter was refloated by the cargo boat at high tide, and taken in tow to the Park Service dock. Underway this evening for Gulf fisheries patrol.

March 12th – 15th — Underway from anchor after sunset on the 11th. Weather laid down nicely. Entered the Gulf of Mexico. No Sanctuary violations. Good! Conservation is the goal. Hopefully our presence is not the only deterrent for the fishing fleet. Good sense, good conscience, good for the planet.

Drifted through the day in the stone crab fields. Miles and miles of water forty to fifty feet deep. The bottom shallows ever so slightly toward the west shore of mainland Florida.

Boarded a shrimper in the Sanctuary. Seemed an honest fellow, just clearing a crab pot caught in his nets.

At night, the fleet stretches out like a string of Christmas lights, north and west, clear of the Zone.

The young ship's officers have learned so much on this trip. I am proud of them, and happy to call them mates.

Feeling like we have done our job, with the shrimpers respecting the sanctuary, departed enroute Cay Sal Bank. Found an ideal anchorage in thirty-five feet. Water clear as glass. We watch starfish and sharks patrol the bottom.

Miami calls, and we are diverted by an aircraft sighting of a possible fast boat, fifty miles south. Another call, never mind, the aircraft tracking the fast-boat had to leave on a search mission. We could never catch them anyway.

Continued to patrol Cay Sal Bank at trolling speed for our final fish call. Caught several barracuda and amberjack. The mood is uneasy, so close to our release home, gone too long. I doubt the worth of the trip, but keep my own counsel.

———————————————

March 17th — Arrive Miami following an overnight steam. No more patrols. Prepared the ship for the voyage home. Took on two new crewmen, fresh from boot camp, while others depart for new duty stations. A short St. Patrick's Day celebration to wrap up the trip, and say farewell to departing sailors. I sent Jack home on emergency leave.

Mood upbeat. A load has been lifted. We will depart in the morning for the Gulf Stream ride to Halifax. Our ultimate destination, as always, Charlevoix.

CAPTAIN'S LOG
GULF STREAM

March 18th — Left Miami at 0900, homeward bound to Charlevoix via Halifax, Nova Scotia, and Niagara, New York. The leg to Halifax is 1380 nautical miles. Gentle easterlies met us in the Gulf Stream. Our trackline lays along the primary axis of the Stream to gain maximum current effect. Recorded fifteen point eight knots through one hour, and averaged better than thirteen knots.

———————   ———————

March 19th — In the early morning, the wind shifted, first west than northeast, directly in our path. I came down with a flu bug, I wish it on no one.

Twenty-five to thirty knot wind on the bow caused progress to slow considerably. Cape Hatteras lives up to its reputation.

———————   ———————

March 21st — A forecast gale arrived from the south, creating a significant sea from abaft the beam. Rolling uncomfortably, but preferable to beating into the waves. If the winds hold for thirty-six hours more, we can surf into Halifax.

A heavy, fresh, rain-shower poured in with the afternoon. Refreshing, but the air and sea begin to turn colder.

———————   ———————

March 22nd — A day's steam from Halifax, we are diverted back south. A tug and manned tow encountering problems with the wind and seas. Their current position 135 nautical miles south and east. The turn met by huge swells on the bow, lucky to make five knots.

Just before dawn, the swells abated. The Tug Kate and Barge Princess have regained control, and are enroute New York City. Came about once more, 408 nautical miles to Halifax.

———————   ———————

March 23rd – 25th — Arrived Halifax on a glassy sea under a clear sky, with the full moon lighting the approach.

Moored alongside the Canadian Forces Naval Yard. Such great support, the Canadians cannot do enough for us. I enjoyed lunch aboard the HMCS Cormorant, a diving research vessel. A glass of beer with the meal. The Canadians whom I have encountered have an interesting picture of the world, seem more in tune to the environment, and more sensitive to the individual. But a hearty lot!

Easter Sunday, March 26th — Underway at 0800. Storm warnings today in the Cabot Straits should blow through by tomorrow. We will ease our way up along the Nova Scotia coast to stay in the lee, then try our hand at a transit of the Gulf of St. Lawrence, and the ice pack, in the morning.

March 27th — Entered the sea-ice pack at dawn, thickness ranges from six inches to three feet or more. Scared off seals who sunned on the floes. Saw a wolf well out in the Strait heading toward shore, he'll be lucky to make it. The day is warmed by a friendly sun as we make fair progress north.

As daylight wanes, our progress is slowed. We will delve into the heavy ice late this night.

BESET

Throughout the day, he had maneuvered the ship through thick piles and chunks and floes, while smaller, thinner ice was crushed by the steel hull. The Captain hadn't slept for nearly fifty hours, since the cutter departed Halifax on Easter Sunday Morning. Two hundred miles off the coast of Prince Edward Island, one wrong turn could prove disastrous, and though he had gained a good deal of respect for his young officers' ability, he found himself unable to share responsibility.

Shortly before midnight, the cutter encountered windrows of ice rafted eight feet above the frozen water surface, and jerked to a stop. A flooding alarm sounded on the bridge. The sound powered phone whistled. The motor room watch reported water leaking into the bilges, apparently from the seal around the propeller shaft. "Recommend shutting down all engines."

$\mathcal{X}$

His father had been much in the Captain's thoughts. So proud to attend the Change of Command ceremony three years earlier, Pop had never really understood the Captain's wanderlust, nor his enlistment in San Francisco. Pop had never served, having been sufficiently high up in the tank-building industry to be considered irreplaceable during World War II. But the Captain had first seen the pride in his father's eyes upon his commissioning ceremony in Yorktown. He'd seen the look again when the children had been born. And he had seen his father's Scot-Irish eyes water, when he had taken command of his own cutter.

When Pop's health failed, the Captain, the youngest, had taken responsibility for his father. He moved Pop to Charlevoix, and the burden had mostly fallen to Glenda and the kids. The ship was often gone. Pop's mind had fallen fast, and the final blessing had arrived a year ago January.

He thought of his Uncle Doug, Pop's younger brother, a war hero who, like so many others, never talked of the war. Doug had written to him in boot camp, the only one who understood. In his late-fifties, with kids of his own, Doug had confided to the Captain, "I'd go again rather than send my kids."

Ironic, he chuckled, to be caught in the ice in these Maritime Provinces, where he and his young wife had visited on their year-delayed honeymoon. Such a happy time. Such a happy place.

He saw his Grandpa Arnold looking down upon him, and knew that he could never hide from his ancestors. And his mother, she must be watching, too.

❦

The Captain left the bridge to meet Bodie below decks in the motor room. Seawater seeped in slowly through the rubber seal surrounding the two-foot diameter, shiny steel propeller shaft. The shaft is turned by the electric motor, which in the diesel-electric plant, receives power from the main diesel generators. The set-up is similar to a train, except that a train doesn't run through water. Water and electric motors do not mix well.

He and Bodie reasoned together. The design must consider a repair option. The seal between the shaft and the hull, located where the shaft enters the water, can only be replaced in dry dock. The engineer poured through the shop manual, and the Captain returned to the bridge.

Moments later, the sound-powered phone whistled again. The seal is inflatable.

Like a car tire that goes flat when the warm summer sun turns to winter cold, the seal had lost pressure. Bodie, and a simple air pump, had solved the dilemma.

❦

Once the engines had come back on line, the cutter made slow progress into the rafted icefield. Still three-hundred miles from the St. Lawrence River entrance, the Captain remained on the bridge until the first light of the day began to ease up from the east. The ice cover lessened, and he instructed the watch to wake him after an hour's rest.

Seemingly moments later, he rolled over in his cabin bunk, still dressed. He looked out the forward port-light, and became confused to see a column of ships ahead, all being led through the ice by a Canadian breaker.

After three stressful days, he had slept for five hours. No one had called.

He climbed to the bridge, where he found LTJG Bills, and the Operations Officer, LTJG Cassidy, together, and calmly in control. "Captain, we decided that you needed some rest."

Of course, he had needed sleep. A brief flash of anger passed quickly, overcome by warm acceptance. Pride swelled in his throat.

His crew had done their job. And he had done his. He had trained them well.

"Carry-on, I'll be below. Shit-on-a-shingle and a couple over easy sound about right. Don't forget the law of gross tonnage."

CAPTAINS LOG
SEAWAY HOME

March 28th — 1800 Navigator's Position Report –

Latitude - 48 degrees 46.7 minutes north, Longitude - 062 degrees 44.3 minutes west.

Underway in the Gulf of St. Lawrence. Took us several hours to work our way out of the ice. Fell in line behind the "Ocean Wind," a salty following the path broken by the Canadian Icebreaker *John A. MacDonald.* Made open water by afternoon.

March 29th — We've seen the last of the sea ice. Entered the mouth of the St. Lawrence River around midnight. Still very wide, eighty nautical miles from land to land. Northerly winds built up before dawn. Some icing but the barometer is rising, the sun begins its ascent, and the river is narrowing. Should pick up the first river pilot by the evening meal.

March 30th — Embarked pilots at Les Escoumins on a clear, cold, and dark night on the eastern reaches of the St. Lawrence River. Lost the port main engine during the night but still made Quebec City by 0800. Repairs made. Changed pilots, and carried on enroute Montreal via Trois Riviere. Boarded a new pilot below the bridge in a snow squall. No visibility for several hours, yet upriver we steamed, fighting the neap tide.

March 31st — Weather cleared twenty miles from Montreal. Moored to the lower approach wall to St. Lambert Lock well after dark. Enjoyed the spectacular lights of Montreal passing in the night. Must wait until morning to lock through, the lock crew is off for the night. We are the first ship, and the Seaway just opened this morning – nighttime passage not allowed.

April 1st — Locked through at 0500. Pilots must have slept in, did not wait. Made U.S. waters by noon, into New York State, and the Ninth Coast Guard District. Continued upstream, locked through Eisenhower and Snell Locks. Spent the night on the lock wall at Iroquois, waiting for daylight, and the lock crew.

April 2nd — Made Lake Ontario by noon, and set two Seaway buoys. Too much ice to put any other aids out for the spring. Set a course for Niagara. Moving along now. As usual, Cleveland wants us to work the Ontario buoys for *Mariposa*, but ice will be around for a couple weeks yet. Much too early to set aids. These folks seem oblivious to the fact that we have been underway for five months, while *Mariposa* sat quietly at the dock in Detroit.

April 3rd — Entered the Niagara River at midnight, and moored at the Coast Guard Station below the fort. Offloaded remnants of the trip, took on fuel and water.

Underway at 0630 and into the first lock in the Welland Canal at 0800. No one ahead of us, we locked through all eight steps, and made Lake Erie by dinnertime. Should arrive at the Detroit River mouth in the morning.

Anxiety is high now — Anticipation grows.

April 4th — Overnight through fog in Lake Erie. Arrived at the Detroit River at 0830. Sun came out and burned off the mist. A warm, pleasant, early spring day as we passed Cobo Hall, and the *Mariposa*, moored alongside in Detroit. On through Grosse Point and Lake St. Clair, by Harsen's Island, Marine City, the St. Clair power plant, and finally, just before dinner, we sailed below the Blue Water Bridge into Lake Huron. Tomorrow the Straights of Mackinac. And home.

CHANGE OF COMMAND

The salty old four-striper pulled on his cigarette, and extended his hand, "Congratulations Tom, you made it. Thought you were too smart. But what do I know? I'm just a tired old sailor."

❧

I have a framed newspaper article on my study wall. The heading reads, "It's home sweet home for the *Mesquite*."

Two photographs are juxtaposed. The upper picture displays the Cutter *Mesquite* moored alongside the Charlevoix City pier. Happy families watch and wave in animated poses. The Cutter shines above, glorious in her presence, with well-earned ribbons and accolades prominently displayed on her super-structure.

The other photograph shows the Captain, having come ashore in civilian clothes, surrounded by his family. He hugs them all at once. Smiles are clear, and contagious, and do not lie.

Glenda has cut her long braid, but her green eyes still sparkle. I hug my daughters, Elsa, who has grown so fast, and Katy, who still clings to her mother. Their faces are bright and clear, and full of promise. James, my son, climbs on a rail to tuck in close. Our children share their mother's happiness.

I see Grandpa Arnold's eyes smiling from my own.

❧

A few months later, as the summer wanes, a new Captain has taken command of *Mesquite*. A time honored ceremony has transferred a complete, and awesome, responsibility.

Several of the once-young officers will go on to command their own ships, in their own times. I share a beer with LTJG Bills, and introduce him to Glenda's little sister. He will one day command a cutter in Charlevoix, and become my brother-in-law, my brother-in-arms.

Grandpa's farm has been lost to the unyielding teeth of urban development. The grassy veranda, where I once sat to consider my future, has become a remnant of my past.

We have built a new farm now, on a broad hilltop in the north woods. My driveway begins where the road ends. Here, I sit on the front porch, and see for miles. Miles gone by, and miles yet to travel, down some new, unexplored path.

I am just another retired Coast-Guardsman, who once was a Captain. I am a wandering soul, who has truly come home from the sea.

CHAPTER FOUR

HOME FROM THE SEA

HALF CORD

Snow squeaks on wooden porch boards
Minus one, sun reflects from white drifts
outdoors, the world is flushed, blushing
invigorated, yet
no stir of wind.
Sweet smell of split maple
Black oval sunflower seeds sink deep below the feeder
Snow melts on hearthstone
from the warmth of the flame
A half cord should last a few days

WILD HORSES

Bryan kick started his dirt bike wearing flip flops. Smoke from the wet engine surrounded him like a mist. He rode up the ramp into the bed of his Chevy pickup, strapped the dirt bike in alongside his Yamaha, and said his farewells. During these few adventurous days, I had enjoyed Bryan's company while riding motorcycles through the Black Hills. But my son James and I, without having to voice our hearts, looked forward to spending some time alone in the Hills, fishing.

"We could hit Spearfish Creek again, or, wait to fish the bigger water with flies later. There's a narrow, deep feeder creek up across the highway I've never tried. Got to be some big ones in there."

"Let's get breakfast and try the little creek with spinners," I replied.

After warming up and devouring left over burritos, we set out in my Tacoma pickup for Hanna Creek. Hanna runs from the Southern Hills in a northerly flow to Cheyenne Crossing, and empties into Spearfish Creek. Hanna's low, grassy banks give trout cover from predators. Using our ultra-light rods and small spinning lures, both James and I caught several small Brown Trout, which had tucked into deep bends, and hid beneath overhanging, black-earth banks. After noon, the fish stopped hitting, so we returned to the cabin for sandwiches and beer, and a siesta.

I rested in a camp chair out behind the cabin, dreamed peacefully in short scenes, and more than imagined the sun warming my face. Cool creek water cleansed my hands, while my thoughts eased into nothingness.

I stirred, cooled, as the sun began a descent through tall spruce into the western ridge on the far side of the canyon. "Hey bud, time to get the fly rods together."

"Son of a Bee-atch' " James replied, rushing into the cabin to find his gear, "I forgot, I need to string a new leader."

I found my canvas rod case in my duffel, fit together my seven and a half foot, four-piece travel fly rod, and fastened on a reel. "I've got an extra nine foot tapered leader if you want it."

James walked out the door carrying his rod, already strung with a tied leader, "Naw, I'm all set."

We laid our rigged fly rods gently into the pickup bed. I drove south a few miles down Spearfish Canyon Road, and pulled over on a narrow shoulder alongside a twenty foot drop off. We looked out on a deep green valley where the creek flattens, before widening into a shallow pool surrounded by swamp grass.

"You go ahead, I'm going to tie a fly on here where I can see what I'm doing."

James bounded down the steep rocky grade effortlessly, and disappeared into a stand of trees. I climbed gingerly, one step at a time. Pieces of flat shale gave way beneath my shoes, and I followed along, as my son moved ahead quietly through waist high long grass. I caught up where he stood on the bank, and he whispered, with his fingers to his lips, "Dad, look. I'm going downstream."

We could see large trout lying in wait, drifting in the slow current twenty yards off shore. I fumbled with my fly, while adeptly, James laid out a cast just upstream of a long, dark shape. A Rainbow, over two feet long, hit his fly. The match was on. The trout fought, leapt shimmering, and twisted toward the freedom of the purple dusk sky. James' hands played the floating line, applied and released tension, the way I had taught him acoustic guitar, naturally, without thought. I watched my son, a man, grow before my eyes, an artist, he landed the fish, and removed the hook. After we admired the prize, he gently returned the trout to the stream. He had overtaken and surpassed me. My son had become the better fisherman. A father's silent prayer answered.

＊

In the evening, we studied topo maps by firelight, and located a stream James had not fished before, where we might find a Brook Trout, rather than the Browns and Rainbows we had been catching. In the morning, after grilled trout and eggs on a toasted tortilla, we were off down the Canyon Road, and turned at Savoy. We passed Roughlock Falls, where we had rested during a bike ride. James had run along the banks to watch fish swim.

A narrow gravel road without a name led further into the unsettled hills. Hidden in the brush, we passed a carved wooden marker, that commemorated the filming of *Dances With Wolves*.

James, desperate to make my stay memorable, and that meant catching fish, pointed out a turnoff, "If this doesn't pan out, I know a mountain lake nearby. But there's a campsite there, and probably a bunch of tourists. I usually go there when Monica wants to swim."

The guidebook had given specific instructions. We just had to recognize the signs and follow the words to Beaver Creek. After fifteen winding miles up into the Hills, the stream passed through a culvert, under the gravel road. The book being true, we found a flat, grassy area to pull off and park the truck. Our instructions were to follow a two-track ranch path for a half mile. Stay on the path to legally cross private land.

On this clear, cool morning, we saw the creek below us as we walked the sparse high country. Above the path, the Hills were covered in long golden grass, and dotted with tall green spruce.

I stopped to breathe in the fresh mountain air, and felt a presence. Scanning the hillside, I noticed we were being watched. Three horses stood high above us, partially hidden, blending naturally into rock outcroppings.

As promised, we found the padlocked gate into National Forest land, and climbed over, using the rusty chain as a step. Beaver Creek, not caring who owned the land, wound through the open valley before us. The Creek ran deep inside six-foot overhanging banks, and cut below the plain of the valley. The terrain varied, and in picturesque bends, shady spruce and cedar lined the banks. A few trees, overturned into the water by wind or erosion, had given texture and character to the stream. In etched, current patterns below obstructions, a light cast would surely find a trout.

A mile or so up the far side of the creek, a sharp bend had been formed by the force of water running focused through a culvert beneath a deserted logging road. Around the bend and below the culvert, Beaver Creek pooled into deep, dark water. James fished the narrows below the pool.

I walked ahead, and laid my lure into a bubbling riffle in the pool, let the spinner float down, and earned my reward. The familiar, prehistoric tug of a Brook Trout pulled me toward the water. I eased the drag until he slowed, then tightened, and drew him in. I looked on like an omniscient god, as released, his muscular shape wiggled away, back into the pool.

James moved up, and stood on a rock beside me on the edge of the pool. Without a word, we took turns casting, and landed a wild Brookie with each toss, for twenty minutes, lost in eternity. Brookies came to us like manna, in pinks and reds and silver flashes. My son and I were bound together in the timeless beauty, and the instinctive struggle of trout.

Fulfilled, I said, " Hey bud, want to hit it?"

"Hell ya, time for a fry bread taco at Cheyenne Crossing."

We began hiking back across country toward the gate. Not just father and son, but friends. James, as always, his head down, searched for critters.

"Hey old man, you just stepped over a snake." And he trotted off to follow the serpent.

Ever since he first walked, James has been fascinated by small creatures of the earth, and treads fearless of bugs, lizards, frogs, and snakes. An adult, but still a beautiful child, he has found his calling, teaching science with passion to young people. His favorite pet, one he's had for twelve years, he calls Norbert. Norbert is a lizard. James followed the snake's probable course, but the long grass made for a trackless trail.

We climbed back over the gate, and walked north along the uneven two-track. As we approached the truck, I noticed the horses I had seen earlier striding slowly, yet purposefully, toward us. I sat on the tailgate to pull off my hip boots, while closer they strolled. I stood, as the dominant horse, a Dun with a dark brown mane, and markings on his legs, stuck his nose in my face. I blew a firm, teasing breath back at his nose.

The other two horses followed the dun's lead. A sorrel with a blond mane, and a bay mare with white markings on her forehead, both sauntered up close to the truck, and poked curiously into the pickup bed.

James, not being too sure about these larger mammals, hurried around to the other side of the truck, putting an obstacle between himself and the mustangs. I called out, "grab the camera" while the dun lifted my waders out of the pickup bed in his teeth. I stroked the sorrel's neck, and yelled playfully at the dun to leave my boots alone. James walked the long way around the truck hood and opened the passenger door to look for the camera. The dun met him at the door, nudged James in the back, and stuck his head in the truck cab, like he knew where the camera was, or maybe wanted to drive.

James, one leg in his waders, the other dragging behind, chortled, "Dad, what the hell?"

I walked around the truck and pushed the bay and the sorrel aside, watching carefully to avoid being stepped on. Laughing so hard that tears dripped down my face, a family trait shared by James, we cry when we really laugh, I shoved the offending dun out of the truck door, feigning complete control. Fortunately, the beast took my fake.

Three shapely, and gentle but wild animals stayed with us for a time, and posed for photographs. Finally, I shooed them away, back to the hills, where they disappeared, blending into the western landscape.

Driving slowly back across the culvert toward civilization, my son and I smiled, kindred spirits, blessed by wild Brook Trout, and three friendly mustangs.

"Now there's something you don't see every day."

PIGEON RIVER

"Insanity: doing the same thing over and over again and expecting different results."
—Albert Einstein

B ranches scraped the pickup as Doc pulled off the gravel road onto a
narrow two track, while daylight waned on a muggy, summer evening. Parked by a gate hidden from the road, we sat on the tailgate, pulled
on our waders, and doped up against the mosquitos. We had a mile and
a half hike in to the old Hemingway cabin, where Doc said, "We have
permission to fish here." But he had no key to the iron gate.

The path wound through heavy woods. Doc and I are the same size,
but I sweated, and struggled to keep up with his long, agile strides. The
woods opened up to an abandoned farm field. I looked down to avoid a
puddle in a depression, and noticed the sign of a bear paw in the mud.
The path closed up again, a tunnel through tight cedar and pines. Finally,
we reached a curved, shallow grade that opened into green, cut grass.
Nestled a few feet from the banks of the Pigeon River, lay a small stone
cabin.

Doc lit up a smoke. I sat on an old wooden bench by the river, and tied
on an Adams, while we waited for the sun to drop just a touch more. The
Adams is a dry fly, a mixture of grey wool and red feathers hiding a tiny
number six hook. Local legend leads us to believe that a certain Judge
Adams, a dedicated fly fisherman, wound this fly for a river in Northern
Michigan back in the 1920's. The evening sky turned a golden pink.
Cedar wax wings traded up and down the river, a good sign.

Doc and I most always split up, and we did again that night. Doc said,
"There's a nice hole around that corner, why don't you wade downstream?" I nodded in concurrence, knowing he wanted to fish a good
hole lying around the bend just upstream.

I slid into the water right in front of the cabin, and loosened up with a
few air casts, which always drives Doc nuts. He generally just waits, smokes,
takes one back cast, and drops the fly gently on the water. Nonetheless, I
laid the line out across the river, and a twelve inch brookie took the fly. I
landed him in long grass by the cabin, and watched in recurrent wonder,
as I released the hook, and the fish wiggled, and swam away.

Doc, wishing he'd chosen downstream, lit another smoke, and watched as I carefully waded across the river, and worked my way down to the first bend. I stopped above a nice riffle current to get my bearings, and balanced on the rocky river bottom.

I blew on the fly to dry it out. Taking the rod back, I anticipated a second trout with my second cast. I concentrated on the surface of the water where I believed a trout would rise, and started to bring my rod forward.

My reverie was ended abruptly by the unyielding tug of my rod tip bending backwards. The hook of the Adams stuck in the branches of a swamp alder that hung off the bank twenty feet behind me.

Frustrated, I shrugged, "Fuck me."

Clumsily, I waded back up the river, reached up to break off the offending alder branch, and retrieved my tangled line and fly. Pissed off, because I probably messed up the hole, it took me a few minutes to straighten out the line, and let the anger wear off.

I worked my way back downstream to cast to the riffle again. I took a deep breath, and let it out slowly. I planned two air casts before landing the fly on the third, right where a trout continued to rise. I pulled the rod back, and as I began forward, a shower of floating fly line and leader fell around my shoulders. The hook was gone.

My Adams, lost in the alder, again.

Not one to be easily defeated, I reeled in the line, eased over to sit on the bank, and lit up a Rum Crook to fight the bugs. After taking a few slow puffs on the cheap cigar, I inspected the line and leader. Both looked fine. I reached into my box to find a replacement for the lost Adams, wiped the sweat from my eyes, put on my crooked reading glasses, and tied on a new fly.

Pleased with myself, and rested, I eased back out into the current. I figured the time taken tying on the new fly had let the hole rest. I found my balance in the stream, and with fresh vigor, prepared to cast.

Just as I raised my rod, Doc called out from the far bank. "Tom, either you're going to have to use less line, or move to a different spot, or you're going to catch that fly in the same fuckin' tree."

I looked up, paused a moment, and replied, "You calling me stupid?"

We got a good laugh, one of those bellyaching, relaxing laughs that lasts a lifetime.

I ended up missing that hole, but caught another small rainbow further downstream. The moon hid behind the clouds. As dark and quiet enveloped the valley, I noticed a foul smell, and a rustling in the bushes on shore. I remembered the bear tracks, and waded back upstream, urgently.

Doc waited at the cabin. He had landed two big brown trout on the upstream bend. He said, "It's after midnight, let's hit it." We hiked back out to the truck, and peeled off our waders.

Doc headed the pickup back west across the Sturgeon River into the town of Wolverine. Disappointment mounted when we found Rocky's Roadhouse closed on this week night. A few miles south on Highway Twenty-Seven, we found another bar, interestingly named, "The Old Twenty-Seven." We bellied up and ordered rum and cokes, and burgers. The place looked empty except for us, and the older lady who set up the drinks. We figured she owned the place. A young guy walked through a swing door, and delivered the burgers, commenting, "She's my mom."

Doc was preoccupied telling the lady the night's fishing story for the first time. He got a good laugh from the lady. Her son, listening in, also smiled at the punch line. I cringed a bit and grinned, the first of many times I would be embarrassed by Doc's telling of this tale.

The son pulled off his apron, and plugged in the Karaoke machine that sat in the corner of the bar. Doc and I finished our burgers to the sound of the son singing the lonesome strains of *Feelings*, while his mother cried.

Doc asked, "Hey, you can sing and play, why don't you give it a try?"

Calmly, I replied, "You calling me stupid?"

DOGS AND OTHER BUDDIES

I buried my buddy's bird dog today.

Doc had flight reservations to Jamaica with his newest version of a woman friend, a lawyer, twenty-two years younger than the Doc. "You should see her beautiful breasts" he says.

I do see her long, curly, blond hair. And the timeless sparkle of the Med in her blue eyes, her staring eyes, clear yet never focused.

The sky is dull and overcast this late April day. Snow is forecast, four to six inches. The world is tired of winter. We should all be flying to Jamaica. But then Doc calls with the news, and asks, "My back is killing me and we're supposed to leave this morning, can you bury Zak?"

&

Zak was a hell of a dog. He ran as fast as lightning. Like most English Setters, he was goofy. He always had a neurotic expression on his dog face that translated into human speak, "Pet me if you like, but I might bite you."

Doc and I hunted birds from the plains of the Dakotas to the thick woods of Northern Michigan. If Doc let him free of the line, Zak would shoot off like a rocket. In a scant few moments, he was on the next ridge a half mile away, chasing some bird or other. His silhouette danced against the horizon. With a long cord attached to his collar, but running free at the other end, Zak was art in motion. With his uncanny sense of smell, he stalked and pointed game birds of many colors, including pheasant, grouse, and woodcock. Back home on a walk in the park, his goofiness prevailed, as he romped, and pointed tweety birds in the park.

&

Chet, my old yellow lab, and Zak's constant nemesis, jumped into the truck on my way to town. The two dogs fought so many times over the years, it was fitting that Chet be present at the end. Most of their altercations were caused when either Doc or I stuck a nose between the dogs, and favored one over the other. Sometimes a fertile bitch would walk by, and naturally, these genuine males strutted to feign dominance.

Over twelve years, measuring eighty-four years each for Zak and Chet, Doc wore out three pickups to my two, as the four of us traveled. October found us in South Dakota for pheasants. In Manitoba, the last week of September, we chased clouds of ducks, and fields of grouse. A weekend, or any available autumn Wednesday, meant a swing to the Upper Peninsula for a partridge in the heavy cover, or just a long country ride.

Zak, with his long, flowing, black and white coat, and Chet, stocky and golden brown, rode side by side in the comfort of a custom-made oak, dual kennel, mounted in the pickup bed. They snarled, sensing the other's presence through the panel separating their dens. We fed and watered them one at a time. Otherwise, Chet would eat Zak's food, while Zak postured and whined. A fight would usually ensue. After twelve years, Doc and I had the routine down pretty well.

I went along on the drive to the breeder in Harbor Springs when Doc first picked up Zak. Doc wanted me to drive home so he could lay on the floor with the pup. Doc slept with Zak in the kennel under his porch for the first week.

His old bird dog, a setter named Jake, died after a long trip out west. The vet called the cause Parvo. I always thought it was the six shot in Jake's backside that he earned for busting out pheasants we had stalked for a mile. The shot didn't kill Jake right away, just slowed him down a bit.

❧

I blew the afternoon off work to put Zak in the ground. I pulled off my blacktop drive, taking the pickup out in the fields for the first time that Spring. Chet loped crookedly alongside the truck. I laid Zak under a choke cherry tree, along an old gray fence line, in an unused corner of my farm. The water table was high, and Zak floated some in the hole, until I covered him with moist, black dirt.

Chet, having some trouble of his own in walking, sat in the long grass nearby, and watched without expression while I covered Zak. A life is gone. Chet knows. Zak is no longer with us. I covered the fresh dirt with a few field stones.

"No more bird dogs," Doc says. "A time comes when you're too old to train another pup."

Time may tell a different story. Things may change when Doc returns home from Jamaica, when these cold April winds turn to the fresh days of September and October, when the world is an autumn field, with a buddy, and a good dog at your side.

I buried my best friend's bird dog today. I still see the look in Doc's eyes when we lifted Zak into my pickup bed.

When a friend asks you to help him with his bird dog, don't ask questions.

OPENING DAY

The evening before the trout opener, Doc and I scouted a small stream flowing under the blacktop a couple bends down from the farm. Almost seventy-two, Doc feels weak sometimes, and likes to fish closer to home.

Snow stayed late this spring, giving hope the water levels would be up, and trout could find a place to hide under overhanging stream banks.

Doc parked his truck by the large culvert where the creek passes below the road. We walked the old railroad grade, and passed pockets of rotting snow and ice on the north slope of small crevices hidden from the sun. The sound of baying hound dogs followed us down the raised, rocky path. Though careful not to slam the doors of the truck, we had spooked the dogs, hidden somewhere in a kennel nearby.

A half mile down the grade, a bridge crosses Orr Creek. The current funneling under the bridge forms a wide pool on the downstream side. Cedar logs, long fallen across the stream in natural chaotic patterns, provide structure for brook trout.

Doc and I looked down from ten feet above, happy to see the water level healthy, and the creek flowing strong. Doc pointed, "Look at that shit-tangle, we'll have to fish with light rods from the bank."

We hiked around the low lying swamp upstream of the bridge, and hunted for spots where a guy could cast without losing a hook. Without our hip boots, we stayed on higher ground, and had to cross over old rusted fences. Fences bent down or broken by years of fishermen who refused to acknowledge the creek as private property.

Satisfied after finding a few promising ledges cut out by the meandering stream, we hiked back down the grade. A backdrop of never-tiring, howling hounds grew louder as we approached the road. "Did you see the "posted" sign?" Doc asked.

"No," I said. I had not seen the sign, and I forgot to look on the way out.

Doc dropped me off at the farm. As he backed out, he rolled down the window and said, "I don't want to get up at the crack of dawn. I'll call you when I wake up or you call me."

I usually rise with the sun, but on this day, rolled over several times for some much needed sleep. Between turns, and short, but effective, restful periods, I looked out the window to a glorious sunny morning. I travelled back to the Saturdays of my youth, waking to a new, clear day, and nothing to do but enjoy the world.

Startled from a dream by the ringing phone next to the bed, I answered, "Hello" in a sleepy, low, gruff voice.

Doc, not a master of cell phones, thought he reached a wrong number, responded questioning, "Hello, Tom?"

After two useless rounds of the conversation, Doc said, "Are you still in fuckin' bed? I'm on my way out from town, get moving."

The face of my old clock radio read nine a.m. The sun had been up since six. I put on the coffee; let Stella, our German shepherd out to run, and lay down on the rug in my study to stretch. Five minutes into stretching, Doc walked in the front door, and called, "Tom?"

Glenda, hardly awakened by the commotion, yelled from bed, "He's in his study."

Doc walked through the living room, and seeing me on the floor in flannel shorts and a tee shirt, said, "I'm going out on the porch for a smoke, call me when the coffee's ready."

Sometime after ten, Doc parked a hundred yards up the road from the creek crossing. We had put on our hip boots before leaving the farm, and quietly began the walk up the grade. Spring peepers sang a symphony from the low lying swampy forest that surrounds the old railroad bed. We heard turkeys gobbling, and then saw a mature tom, with a long-hanging wattle, hiding in the woods. Halfway to the bridge, the hounds joined the band.

About forty feet before reaching the bridge, Doc said, "Let's get our rods ready here."

We tiptoed slowly to the edge of the concrete that frames the bridge culvert. Doc smiled, "Go ahead, take the first cast."

I laid a panther martin perfectly into the current, and let it float down to a small pool formed by a downed cedar tree, and slowly reeled back the swimming spinner.

Nothing.

Doc cast, also with no luck. Both of us knew the likelihood of a brook trout hitting diminished directly with the number of casts into a pool. We alternated for a few minutes. "I might have had a bite," he called, our spirits rising.

Wanting to test the new knee I had installed ten weeks earlier, I climbed down the bank, leaving the broad pool for Doc to fish from above. I worked my way downstream fishing little runs where the creek narrowed, and spots where the current undercut the bank. Somewhere in my head, I knew the stream was too cold, that we were too early in the year, and too early in the day. The sun needed to warm the water, and wake the trout. But I still pushed downstream, careful not to stumble on exposed roots, my face slapped by wayward bushes along the bank. I waded across, and found a large bend. "A trout must live here," I thought, but an empty cast disappointed again.

On the other bank, I found a clearer path to walk back to the bridge. Doc was gone, I figured maybe a half mile upstream, around the swamp where we walked the previous evening. I climbed down the bank on the upstream side. I could fish my way along the creek, and likely run into him.

Continually caught by pine branches and bushes in the snarly swamp, I looked for a place to enter the water. I spotted a green grass ledge, and while slowly pulling a fresh, reddish-purple tag alder strand out of the way, paused, and noticed the first fuzzy, grey bud of spring, just inches from my eyes.

I stepped into the water. The cool spring run sucked the legs of my hip boots against my jeans like a soothing compress. I saw a small creek, about eight feet wide, entering the main stream just ahead. I realized that this was Skinner Creek, which drained the land for several miles to the northwest, including the tiny trickle flowing through my farm. I had named the water Black Creek, after the oozing, black bottom. Following a romp in the rich soil, my old yellow lab, Chet, would wander home, his legs covered in dark muck.

I worked slowly upstream following Skinner Creek, and struggled to fit through tight trees. Whenever I looked down for a place to step, I caught the hook of the Panther Martin on a hanging branch, and took some time to set it free. I came to an island outcrop in the center of the creek that divided the water into two flows. One side turned, and cascaded like a miniature waterfall. The far side flowed in a straight run. The two met again ten feet downstream, where a cedar tree shaded the rejoined waters.

I took a deep breath, certain that this bend would hold a brook trout. I dropped the lure into the water, and let out a few feet of line to tempt any fish living by the bank near the cedar. I saw a sliver flash and felt a tug, then a release. I reeled in, and dropped again, several times, and each time, he tugged, and then let go. I saw he was a small trout, not a legal keeper, but at least I had felt a tug on this opening day.

I hiked back out of the creek bottom, saw Doc sitting on the ground by the bridge, and plopped down next to him. I bummed a smoke, and we swapped stories. I told him about my one bite. He said, "I thought you'd wade to the log bridge upstream."

Turning to his creel, Doc pulled out two speckled, fifteen inch brook trout, and said, "I got them both below the log bridge."

Astonished, happy for Doc, but frustrated, I could only reply, "Wow."

We talked awhile before Doc reached back in the creel, and lifted out the two trout. The fish seemed a little dull in color, then he turned one, and I saw that it had been cleaned.

Smiling slyly, Doc said, "I took them out of my freezer this morning."

Laughing like kids on a Saturday morning, we walked back down the railroad grade to the waiting truck. We stopped several times to listen to the turkeys gobble, and tried to spot them in the woods.

I turned and saw the yellow "Posted – No Trespassing" sign attached to a worn tree stump.

The hounds howled, while we sat on the tailgate, and pulled off our hip boots.

CHET'S GONE

Chet died in the garage while I slept.

We both knew death was coming. These past few weeks he barked for no apparent reason. He barked at the silence, the only sound his old ears heard. He barked at the moon and the stars. He barked to keep demon death at bay.

The previous Saturday, I turned the garden soil, as I do each spring. A renewed struggle to keep weeds away until the sweet corn comes. For twelve years, Chet watched and waited as I worked. He liked to lie on the grass by the edge of the garden until the sun grew too hot, and he found shade and cooler grass under the north eave of the house. But he always watched me work. He knew something good would be coming, but I don't think he knew when.

He ate vegetables. Tomatoes and cukes mostly. Some people say dogs are color blind. I doubt it. He knew when the tomatoes turned red. He knew when the cukes were fresh and green.

Chet was sneaky, always thought he was fooling me. He timed his raids strategically. He waited until I was out on the front porch, or away from the farm. One windy day, winding my truck home up the long drive, I was greeted by corn stalks and silk spread across the lawn. He left half eaten cobs of sweet, raw corn, perfectly ripened; a cucumber mush with one bite taken, and mashed, partially eaten tomatoes strewn about, seeds everywhere. Volunteer plants and more weeds would soon follow. Chet knew how mad I was inside, and cowered with a helpless innocent look that betrayed his lying thoughts, "I'm just a dumb dog. I don't know any better."

A few days later, I would return home to a similar scene, and all I could do was smile, and pick up corn silk.

Chet liked to wander, and I generally didn't worry too much. Except in the fall, when brain dead, down-state deer hunters were around. From a distance, he could be mistaken for a small doe. A bullet from a high powered rifle can travel a mile. Then there are coyote hunters who poison deer carcasses. Chet loved a good carcass.

I knew his time was near. He hadn't wandered lately, staying too close by the door. He seemed lost, not knowing what to do. Doggie Alzheimer's maybe? He barked even though he couldn't hear himself. The porch boards would shake with his thunder. "Why the hell am I barking?" he must have thought, "because that is what I do. Maybe I can conjure a car up the drive, like the old days."

The last year or so he had trouble climbing steps. Chet and I came up with a solution. I called him over, and he pointed his snout up the stairs. I would reach my arms around his tail end, barely touching his crank, while avoiding it at the same time. He kind of liked it, and turned with a sardonic smile. I lifted his back legs while he walked up the steps with his front. Our own four-legged wheel barrow race.

Chet was a strong swimmer. He used his tail as a rudder. When he was less than a year old, just a pup, Doc and I were up in Manitoba hunting ducks. Chet took to retrieving so well it was scary. I didn't really train him; he was born an innate, natural retriever.

I knocked down a canvasback with four shot from my over/under. The duck wasn't hit too badly, and floated out in the ten-knot river current. Chet jumped in. Ten months old, and not nearly strong enough for these conditions, I thought. By the time he reached the thunder duck, they were eighty yards downstream. The duck dove under the surface. Chet followed, taking three breaths, three times up, and down again. On the last rise, he had the canvasback in his mouth, and began the swim back up current. I watched anxiously, as time dragged. Finally, there he was at the marshy shore by my blind, and he dropped the duck at my feet. Wet and wagging, Chet smiled. I never worried about him much after that, that is, until these past few weeks.

There was no one to stretch with this morning, no one to wander in, and lie down next to me. No loose skin, nor fur to stroke. No earthy goodness to smell. No thick tail to whack me while he wagged like a helicopter.

Chet, the only dog that was ever really just mine, made me young again. He simply knew more than I could ever teach. He was simultaneously tame and wild. Truly, a water dog, a yellow lab more light brown, with coffee dark streaks in his coat.

I buried Chet down by the fence line, under a shady tree, next to Zak.

They say dogs are like their owners. I hope so.

LAST CALL

I sat at my desk and scratched my swollen little finger until it ached. Poison was held hostage inside my skin. A yellow and black bee had stung me while I reached beneath layers of grape leaves. I had quickly dropped the plucked grapes into a pan, yelled, "Fuck me" to no one in particular, and run into the house for an ice cube to sooth the sharp pain.

I hadn't fished on Sunday. The grapes hung purple, ready for the crock. My fingers throbbed from kneading and popping the thick skins from the gel fruit. A second bee stung me just before dying when I tried to crush him in a towel at the sink. My middle finger slipped, and with his last act on this earth, instinct for self-preservation prevailed. Another ice cube melted into water.

∝

Monday, the final day of trout season, snuck up on me, a robber come knocking at the door. An early morning fog hung in the lowlands below the cool rising sun. This last day of September promised dry, cool temperatures, enough to still the biting bugs. The headwaters of the wild and scenic Jordan River lay a short twenty minutes away. The river called.

The fishing season had been good to me. Since the late April opener, many trout had given themselves up in many different streams. All, save two for a breakfast one hungry morning, had been returned to the healing waters whence taken.

I fought a three foot Spanish mackerel for over half an hour while standing on the bow of a rented boat, anchored in a scenic inlet between the Gulf of Mexico and the Intercostal Waters of Florida.

In the Black Hills, I had watched my son James grow into an expert angler, a kindly master of trout. We landed Browns, Brookies, and Rainbows, and talked deep into mountain nights.

I landed small mouth bass where the water of the Point aux Chenes River flows in a large bend, and merges with Lake Michigan. Seven casts produced seven fish on the Fourth of July. I returned on Labor Day and realized, standing in the river, that someone had cracked fourteen inches off my ultra-light rod by sitting in the back seat of my pickup, where no one usually sits, because my gear is stored there. I stuffed the broken end into the rod base section and cast anyway, aiming forty inches of remaining graphite with surprising accuracy. I landed three nice bass with the broken rod.

I ate salmon fresh from the Big Lake during the mid-August run, and just a few days earlier, lunched on a Brook trout caught in the rusty, but clear iron waters of the Escanaba River. I had nothing to prove, and only failure to gain, yet water called me one last time.

Two other cars were parked by the steel gate. I lit a smoke, one of just two I had left, swearing again that I'd quit, and walked around the gate, up the path to the Pinney foot bridge. Looking downstream, I saw one fisherman busy tying a rig. I planned to fish upstream, so returned to the pickup, and pulled on my hip boots. A man and woman and two black labs romped on the path to the sandy parking area. Partridge season had opened in mid-September, and I greeted them while petting the labs, "See any birds?"

The man smiled, "Nope, nothing," and they piled into a big blue Ford truck.

The Jordan headwaters are formed by the confluence of many small streams that flow together in a myriad of angles, through a deep, dark lowland forest. Once I left the path to the footbridge, I entered a foreign country. I splashed through a couple of deep runs, almost tripping on protruding roots. I grabbed overhanging cedar branches for balance. On a piece of solid ground, I sprayed my hands and arms with Bull Frog, a child safe, deet-free bug dope with SPF 30 protection, and a surprisingly pleasant smell. One whiff awakened me from a daydream, and I returned from my vision of the deep winter snow soon to come. I took off my hat, and sprayed a dose around the inside band.

I worked my way back toward the main river about forty yards below the bridge. The river was high, and running fast for autumn. These woods are ultra-light country, much too close for a fly rod. Cedar branches hang without symmetry, and grab lines and hooks with green boughs. I had found a new rod, and screwed on my old trusty reel, though the broken rod still hung in the back window of my truck. Might need a spare.

I laid an orange and silver Panther Martin lure into the current, felt a hit, a bump, and a release. A trout had considered my offering, and thought better. I hiked slowly upstream, walking along the edges, and took a few casts at each likely hole.

The sun joined the day, filtered occasionally through trees, and sparkled on the stream. Shadows cast by cedars along the bank became indistinguishable from logjams, and bobbing, black branches. The river came alive.

Wandering against the flow, and concentrating on the water, I looked up just before bumping into the other fisherman I had seen from the bridge. He was still, or again, tying on something, but now on the other side of the bridge. He must have crossed while I petted the labs. I said, "Sorry, are you fishing upstream?"

"No. I'm about done. Any luck?"

"Naw, just one hit down by the bridge," I replied, walked wide around him, and skipped several holes to create some space.

After resting a moment, I realized that the lure wasn't working, and tied on a little silver pattern, with pink and blue markings and black dots, made to look like a fingerling trout. Instead of casting and reeling in, I let the new lure ride and spin in the current just above a downed log. A familiar deep tug awakened my senses. I worked the fish around the downfall, and into the air. An eight-inch Brown trout. I'd brought my phone for the camera, and captured a nice shot before placing the fish back into the stream. I wet my hands, and cool water ran through my fingers.

I continued walking the edge, and cast at each hole for a mile or so, until I hit Landslide Creek, then worked the feeder stream up a few hundred feet. On my second cast, my trout colored lure grasped a sunken log. I thought, "Probably deeper than my hip boots are high, but I want that lure back."

I rolled up my shirt sleeve, and plopped down in a beaver slide, while feeling for the creek bottom with the sole of my boots. The ground felt reasonably solid, so I stepped in, waded to the middle, reached down into the water, and freed the hook.

Standing in the current, I realized that I had come for the water, for the feel of the fresh, cool stream on my skin, for the sun warming my wet arm and hands, to feel the water disappear into the sunlit air.

I decided to push on to find a place to cross the main stream, so that I could walk the opposite bank back to the bridge, and find somewhere

I had not been before. I walked and cast, and searched upstream for a shallow crossing. I heard a noise across the river, held a cast and looked. Deer might be crossing, I thought, hopefully, knowing that bears hadn't yet hibernated for the winter.

A resounded thrust. A whoosh echoed through the woods like a jet airplane. I looked up to see the underside of a blue heron's wings just feet above my head.

I had walked much farther than I planned, at least a mile deeper into the wild, and still found no shallow place to cross. I heard a duck quacking in my pocket. Doc was calling on the cell phone. I told him I was trying to find a place to cross. He warned, "Be careful. That's why they call it Landslide Creek. Quicksand dumps into the river there."

"I'll remember that."

I turned back once, momentarily disoriented, but found my bearings, and continued upstream. Finally, I came to a wide, flat expanse of sand and gravel, and nosed my hip boots into the muck by the bank. After I slid a few inches, the bottom held. I worked across the river slowly, step by step, over gravel and small boulders that tried to turn my ankles.

I climbed up on the far bank, and entered a magical, emerald green world. Midday, but dark, as the sun could not penetrate the leaves. High ceilinged cedars grew out of spongy, moss covered ground, where I paused to rest, and laughed, thinking about leprechauns.

I had planned to fish this far side walking downstream, back to the bridge, and perhaps reach runs that had been out of casting range on the way up. But here, nature protected the stream from man. Overhanging branches prevented me from taking my rod back.

I crossed several small feeder creeks, and lost sight of the main river. I started sweating, and hiked quickly through the deep deer swamp, with only an occasional glimpse of the Jordan sparkling in the sun. My throat was parched. Water surrounded me, but I had brought none to drink. I considered tasting the river, but the fear of Guardia stopped me.

I relaxed only after spotting the foot bridge. I walked to a grass perch for a final few casts. Looking down, two huge salmon glided in the clear, waist deep water, one spawning, one chasing. I dabbled the lure, and the male, the chaser, was momentarily interested, moving ever so slightly away toward the disturbance, the color, before being drawn back to his spawning target.

I climbed onto the bridge, repeating to myself, "one more, one more cast."

I walked over the bridge, and looked downstream to where I'd seen the other fisherman when I first arrived. I climbed down off the bridge, worked further downstream, and stopped to try a spot. "Just one more cast," I repeated loud enough for only myself to hear, knowing that the large salmon had disrupted the small water, and spooked the trout.

"Last call."

I tossed the pink and blue lure to the far shore, and reeled. I watched the shiny spinner clear underwater logs, float gently in the current, then hold, and twirl above a beaver dam upon reaching the extent of the line I had let out.

And the primeval tug. A young trout pulled for his life.

I brought him in, and held the fish in my outstretched hand. I freed the hook from his mouth and returned the speckled, under aged Brook Trout back into the stream. The healing water flowed, covering my hands.

The trout swam away, safe until spring.

EPILOGUE

LOOKING FOR LOST PLACES

I sat struggling at my desk, fighting conflict and my stubborn streak, reading reviews of a recent story. I heard the phone ring, but ignored the interruption. Doc was on the line, and shouted into the answering machine loud enough that I heard the message two rooms away, "The woodcock should be coming in up by the Straits. Pookie is in the kennel. Give me a holler if you still want to go."

He called last night in a funk, and cancelled. We had made plans to drive north to an old favorite spot we hadn't hunted for maybe half a dozen years. Doc said he wanted to drive. But his on again off again, much younger lady friend had put him into a spiral. Doc retired from active practice, but will never retire from taking care of other people. From the frustrated tone of his voice on the answering machine, I knew he needed to get away, into the woods.

I stewed at my desk, wondering why these critics always want more of me. Maybe I misinterpreted the comments, read through too fast. Why can't they read in between the lines? Fuck it, I'm going hunting.

I called Doc back, "I'll be in to your place by noon."

He replied, "Pook's in my truck, I'll drive."

I parked in Doc's driveway in town. Dakota, alias Pookie, Doc's female yellow lab, looked out from the kennel in the bed of his truck. I walked into the house. Doc sat on the couch trying to decide which pair of boots to wear, "I've got to take a crap before we go."

"Hurry the fuck up, the birds will fly south before we get to the Straits. We can stop on the road."

"Ya, OK, I'll drive, Pook's already in the kennel," Doc replies.

I smiled, thinking, *Third time you told me.*

Heading north across the Charlevoix drawbridge, I lit a smoke, and one for him, and watched carefully. Driving is an effort that takes both of us these days, to stay out of trouble. We settled in silence for a time, then Doc asked, "Did I tell you about the Krauthammer interview?"

He launches into a history of Charles Krauthammer's life without waiting for a reply. I listened, watched the fading fall colors pass by, and kept an eye on the Gazateer to make sure we didn't miss a turn.

Ten minutes later, somewhere in the hills near Bliss, Doc paused to breathe. I said, "You told me this yesterday. If his father was from the Ukraine and his mother from Belgium, and he was born in Brazil, how the hell can he be American?"

Doc paused before backtracking, "Maybe he was born in New York. I ordered his new book."

We parked the truck, and walked on the bridge over the Maple River. Just something we do, stop at bridges, and stare into stream waters running below. Might see a trout. Doc pointed upstream into an endless swamp of black water and tag alders, "Next spring, we should bring a canoe, and paddle upstream. There must be some big brook trout living up there."

"I've heard the swamp is full of snakes."

Doc leaned his head back, and with squinting eyes, asked "Did I ever tell you this one?"

"I was fly-fishing on the Jordan one time, wading by the power line. A couple young guys came by in canoes, catching water snakes, balling them up, and tossing them back and forth between canoes. Two old ladies were paddling behind them, and smiling with curiosity, asked me, "What are those boys throwing?""

"Snakes."

The old ladies beached their canoe, left it in the woods, and hiked a half mile through the swamp to the Webster Bridge."

Back in the truck, I searched the map, trying to find the cross road where we had hunted partridge some years before. I commented, "When was the last time we were up here, twelve years? Krauthammer must have extra sensory perception. I think that he applies his lost sense of touch and feel to his brain, like blind people, like musicians, like Ray Charles or Stevie Wonder."

We took turn after wrong turn, followed the dotted mile squares printed in the Gazateer, and searched for something familiar, an edge of trees, or a field of waving wild grasses. Nothing looked the same. Sensing the first fingers of frustration, I became resolved, and studied the names of the dirt roads, hoping to tweek my memory.

Another habit we've developed, we never give up on a word or a name.

"Try alphabetically," Doc spouts, "Let's see, A.., B.., C, Carp River Road?"

"Nope," I reply, "D..?" We know that if we give up trying, all will be lost.

We passed a prefab ranch house, and I point out, "That wasn't here before."

Doc, agitated, "Everything is fucking posted. Can't you tell State land from the map?"

"No. They changed the key. Public land is supposed to be shadowed light green but the whole State of Michigan is light green. Turn left here, on Ball Road."

We made our way west along a gravel road. I looked ahead, where the road rose up a gentle grade after passing through a wetland. A deep memory worked through the fog in my mind. "This is it."

Doc replied, "I'm not too sure" as we drove past a new building and a sign, indicating *Ottawa Band of Chippewa, Recreation Center,* "Look, the Tribe built tennis courts."

A thought flushed through my mind like a bird in front of the windshield. *How many years ago, with young dogs, now dead, had Doc and I walked this wetland woods? Partridge busted from berry bushes, startling and shaking our then young nerves. I get a shot off, the beautiful walnut grain of my Browning over/under 20 gauge smooth in my deer skin gloves. A couple plump birds cleaned, stuffed with shallots, and slow roasted for dinner.*

We drove past a turnoff with a rough stone surface. I recognized a pile of gravel a few hundred feet off the road at the end of a logging trail. I repeated, "That's it."

Doc continued driving up the main road, both sides marked with *No Trespassing* signs every forty feet. I said, "Turn around." We drove back slowly, and together, watched birds flush through our memories from hidey-holes hidden in days past, and silently, we cursed each sign.

Further along the road, Doc spotted an old man, raking leaves in his yard, which was surrounded by dense stands of maple and aspen. Doc pulled over to the side. I stuck my head out of the window as the man, dressed in jeans and a blue flannel shirt, laid down his rake, looked relieved, and walked toward the truck.

"Looks like a lot of work. Lucky we came by, you could use a break."

"You got that right," he replied, offering me the rake handle in jest.

"Say, we hunted here years ago, and we're trying to find a spot where a trail leads past a gravel pit, then turns into a logging road with young popple trees along the edges. I thought that might be the spot over on Ball Road. Is that State land?"

He leaned on the window, grateful for the break in action. "That section used to be public, now belongs to Fred Jackson. I don't know if he's around today."

"You know of any State land for bird hunting?"

"Haven't hunted birds for fifteen years. Had a stroke last year. Told myself to let these leaves alone. But then I got started, and you know the wife, she's off at work and what do I do?"

"Yah, I cleaned up my yard yesterday."

Doc laughed, "Not me."

The old gent showed me a place on the map in a swampy area that drained into Douglas Lake. Reluctantly, he pushed his weight off the door, and with a wave, returned to several large piles of golden leaves.

My mind wandered, "Krauthammer seems like he's all head, an omniscient being, a floating head, who speaks down to mere mortals waiting below. He must get frustrated on those panels, listening to the other idiots rant."

Doc replied, "I think he has some feeling in his arms. He squeezes a tennis ball in his hand sometimes. You know he was liberal in his younger years. What's that Churchill quote about liberals with a heart and conservatives with a head? I told my daughter that yesterday, she said she'd rather have a heart than a brain."

I directed Doc six miles, to the spot on the map the old man had suggested, "I don't think Churchill said that. You know, I'm rediscovering my liberal bent."

"What d'ya mean, you must have smoked too much marijuana in college?"

"I believe that we have a responsibility to take care of those who truly can't take care of themselves."

Doc, incredulous, begins to form a follow-up question, but before he can, I interrupt, "The operative word is *truly*."

A muddy and sand road led along the shore of a small lake. We passed by several seasonal cabins before turning west into a tunnel of overhanging trees. Doc pulled over, got out, and walked back into the woods, his morning coffee finally kicking in. "Don't let Pook out. Remember what happened with Zak."

A few rusty oak leaves still clung to grey branches. *Zak, Doc's old English Setter, had rolled in Doc's mess, so Doc tossed him in a cold October lake, like the one we had just passed. Zak spent the rest of that hunt in the kennel. Hunting dogs are named in one syllable, with hard consonants. Easier for them to remember.*

We pulled back onto the seasonal road. Bright orange, stick-on, posted signs began appearing again, marring trees, staring like jack o' lanterns, warning away all who might dare to enter.

Doc said, "Let's hit it. We can stop at the Frontier Bar for a beer and a chicken sandwich. I was hoping to marinate some woodcock breasts, and roast them with water chestnuts wrapped in bacon. You know, I think Charles Krauthammer would trade lives with me in a heartbeat."

"Probably," I replied, filling in thoughts between the lines, like Krauthammer stuck in a wheelchair out in these woods, and Doc and me, looking for lost places.

ACKNOWLEDGEMENTS

To my readers – please remember that these are my stories. Some names have been changed. Some characters may be a combination of people, or an approximation of my memory.

For my wife of forty-four years, Glenda Catherine (McCarty) Conlan, who always kept the home fires burning. The sketches you have seen throughout the book are hers. Glenda has always been a talented artist, so much more so than I.

For our children, Elsa, James, and Katy, and their life-partners, Josh, Monica, and Sean. And, mostly for my grandchildren, Grady, Zeke, and Walker. Their hope is our hope.

Many friends and fellow writers have helped me with this project. Please forgive me if I fail to mention you, it is my memory, not your help, that fails.

The Doc' — Bill Mosher, my friend, first reader, critic, and the source of most of what is funny herein. Becky Bills, another early reader, and Chet's other best friend.

My sister, Jill Andrea, who has always encouraged and supported me. My brother-in-law and early mentor, Al Masarik. Al has passed, but lives on through his poignant poetry. My big brother Dennis, who always said I was smarter, but we know the truth.

Thanks to my fellow writers at Queens — Michael Brantley, Annie Fitzmaurice, Meghan Florian, Donna Kaz, Rikki OsBourne, Donna Brooks, and Mardi Link. Also my mentor writers at Queens — Emily Fox Gordon, Cathy Smith Bowers, Peter Stitt, Jim McKean, and Jon Pineda.

Many thanks to Betty Henne for her help in editing. Please forgive my fragments — however intentional!

And to the folks at Mission Point Press, Heather Shaw and Doug Weaver, who helped my vision come true.

— 179 —

I would like to thank, and credit the following publications where my stories have appeared in print.

"Sandhill Cranes and Wine" — *QU Literary Journal,* Volume IV. Finalist for the Annie Dillard Prize, Bellingham Review.

"Dogs and Other Buddies," "Chet's Gone" (Chet Trilogy) — *Puppy Love Anthology* 2015.

"Opening Day" — *Tulip Tree Review,* Volume I.

"Pigeon River" — *The Water Holds No Scars: Fly Fishing Stories of Rivers and Rejuvenation.*

"Floating Dawn" — *Vine Leaves Literary Journal.*

"Fawn" — *The Avocet,* Fall 2016.

"My Journey Begins Where the Road Ends…" — Queens University of Charlotte, MFA Thesis.

ABOUT THE AUTHOR

Tom Conlan lives, writes, and tends his grape vines at Blackcreek Farm in the highlands of Northern Michigan.

He has captained a Coast Guard Cutter, sailed the world's lakes and oceans, and now searches for the elusive brook trout in backwater streams.

Tom's work has appeared in print in *Vine Leaves Literary Journal, Issue #12*, in the print *Anthology, Puppy Love*, in *Tulip Tree Review*, in the anthology, "The Water Holds No Scars," and in *Qu Literary Review*. His work was chosen as a finalist for the Annie Dillard Prize in the *Bellingham Review*.

Tom attended the Iowa Writer's Workshop, holds a Master of Fine Arts in Creative Writing from Queens University of Charlotte, and a Master of Science from the US Naval Postgraduate School in Monterrey, California.